A Tale of Three Fish

A TALE OF THREE FISH

A Lifetime of Adventures Chasing Atlantic Salmon, Steelhead, and Permit

JIM STENSON

STACKPOLE BOOKS

Essex, Connecticut
Blue Ridge Summit, Pennsylvania

STACKPOLE BOOKS
An imprint of Globe Pequot, the trade division of The Rowman & Littlefield Publishing Group, Inc.
4501 Forbes Blvd., Ste. 200
Lanham, MD 20706
www.rowman.com

Distributed by NATIONAL BOOK NETWORK

British Library Cataloguing in Publication Information available

Library of Congress Cataloging-in-Publication Data
Names: Stenson, James, 1957– author. Title: A tale of three fish : a lifetime of adventures chasing Atlantic salmon, steelhead, and permit / by Jim Stenson.
Description: Essex, Connecticut : Stackpole Books, [2023] | Summary: "Author Jim Stenson chronicles his life of adventures chasing the holy trinity of fish: permit, steelhead, and salmon"— Provided by publisher.
Identifiers: LCCN 2023030310 (print) | LCCN 2023030311 (ebook) | ISBN 9780811772501 (paperback) | ISBN 9780811772518 (epub)
Subjects: LCSH: Fishing—North America. | Fishing—Anecdotes. | Atlantic salmon fishing— North America. | Steelhead fishing—North America.
Classification: LCC SH441 .S817 2023 (print) | LCC SH441 (ebook) | DDC 639.2097—dc23/ eng/20230822LC record available at
https://lccn.loc.gov/2023030310LC ebook record available at
https://lccn.loc.gov/2023030311

∞™ The paper used in this publication meets the minimum requirements of American National Standard for Information Sciences—Permanence of Paper for Printed Library Materials, ANSI/ NISO Z39.48-1992.

A Tale of Three Fish *is dedicated to my wife, Sandra, who spent long hours editing, formatting, and trying to understand the vernacular of fly fishermen. Even though I know deep down that you enjoy helping me write, I love you exponentially more than you love me! I couldn't have done it without you.*

CONTENTS

Acknowledgments

It's almost impossible to thank everyone who contributed to this book. Most of my friends have no idea of the role they played in my life. Some have passed. Some are hanging on by a thread. Others seem to have found the fountain of youth. Still others continue to fish and mark the day not by how many fish they catch but by the memories of a time long gone.

Still, in the end, it's always been my closest friends and family that provide the opportunity for me to write. None are more important than my wife Sandra and my close friends like Walt Winton, Norm Zeigler, and Alan Kennedy.

Then others, like Steve Kantner, warned me of the trials and tribulations facing writers and journalists in a time when instability is the norm, not the exception. Of course, I didn't know it then, but Steve was right on so many levels. Harry Middleton once wrote: "A writer may write alone, live alone, but sooner or later he must get up from his desk, leave his garret. When he does, he is more likely out of his element, an awkward sort. So it is with me. Such a writer needs all the help he can get. I have had more than my share."

No truer words have rolled off the tongue of the writer, and like Harry Middleton, I have had more than my share of help along the way.

Introduction

We have reached the time in the life of the planet, and humanity's demand upon it, when every fisherman will have to be a river-keeper, a steward of marine shallows, a watchman on the high seas. We are beyond having to put back what we have taken out. We must put back more than we take out.

—Thomas McGuane

Some of us must have done something right in a previous life, allowing us to profit from the opportunity to travel the world and chase some of the greatest gamefish on the planet. But, unfortunately, it's an opportunity rarely bestowed on the young. I was fortunate, even though I don't cherish looking back at the old pictures of me grinning with unwarranted pride next to a pile of dead fish.

As the years fade, I find less enjoyment in focusing on quantity and instant gratification. Instead, I revel all the more in the travel itself, in nature pure and untamed, and in the relationships that develop with my travel companions and with the local characters that give each place its unique flavor.

The following pages contain a collection of essays about three species of gamefish dear to my heart. For full disclosure, I am just as enamored with the environments in which they live and the diversity thereof. For instance, although I confess myself a die-hard saltwater junkie who spent most of my life in the brine, two of the "tails" described in this tome belong to anadromous fish. Because of my briny childhood, I didn't discover steelhead until my late teens. Many years later, I succumbed to the challenge of Atlantic salmon.

Not to leave out my first love entirely, I end with accounts of my many attempts (and rare successes) to catch a permit on the fly. Even though I freely admit I will fish for almost anything, anytime, deep in my heart I have long considered permit the Holy Grail of gamefish, not least of which because I love the environments in which permit live—who doesn't? I love the sensation of standing on the deck of a flats boat pitching flies to giant permit on a pristine flat in a mangrove-choked estuary of Central America or the Florida Keys. I remember with almost perfect clarity the spiritual awakening, the epiphany, the moment I finally realized how ridiculous it was to think I could hoodwink a permit with a twisted piece of steel, two lead eyes wrapped with fluorescent green thread, and few pieces of 1960s shag carpet.

Floating down the Grand Cascapédia in late summer in an old Atlantic salmon canoe, searching for the eponymous piscine adversary, evokes a similar mix of joy, deep relaxation, and self-deprecation related to the probable futility of the outing. The float in late summer and early fall remains nothing short of breathtaking, riverbanks lined with trees ablaze in intense reds, bumblebee yellows, and mango browns. All around, mergansers are dragging strings of ducklings up and down the river, and kingfishers work diligently on chasing fishermen away from the shoreline where their hungry chicks keep them on the hop. Our quarry, the Atlantic salmon, is meanwhile waiting, stacked in the deep pools, for the seasons to change, anxious to move up the river and spawn. At some point, we begin to realize why we made the long journey in the first place. Then you realize it's not the fish you're after. It's the experience.

As if God were a fisherman, the Atlantic salmon season starts to peter out when the steelhead fishing in British Columbia is beginning to heat up. The Skeena drainage is vast. The names of the rivers that feed the Skeena read like a who's who of wild steelhead rivers. Given a chance, I would fish all of them. Hell, given the opportunity, I would live there, but if I had to pick the ultimate river and time of year, the Morice River in late October and early November would take the prize. Bouncing your way up and down the Morice in a jet sled in search of winter steelhead is a life-changing experience. The Morice River is one of the best (if not the best) late-season steelhead rivers on the planet. Regardless of the number of relatively large grizzly bears. Mother Nature does her best to keep you occupied.

At its core, this book is about long, slow road trips, Mother Nature, mom-and-pop diners, colorful characters, friendships developed over time, and the tremendous amount of after-dinner cocktails shared with your comrades. It's about the eighteen-year-old Scotch we guzzle down and the lies we tell around the campfire.

Finally, it's about appreciating what's left. If we take a deep breath and relax, the world will, at least for a few moments, let us remember the way it was and, with the right attitude, can be again.

"*Carpe diem, quam minimum credula postero.*" (Pluck the day, trusting as little as possible in the future.) —Horace

Time and tide wait for no man!

My God, Bones, What Have I Done?

It was 1974. I was seventeen years old and hell-bent on fly-fishing the Great Northwest for steelhead. Three weeks earlier, I had left Sarasota, Florida—just pulled out of my parents' driveway and pointed the Bronco north by northwest. I knew where I wanted to end up, but other than that, I had no preconceived plan. Except one! I dearly wanted to catch a steelhead on a fly. I was flying by the seat of my pants. Considering I was only wearing a pair of shorts, a worn-out T-shirt, and a pair of flip-flops, I didn't have much to fly by. In the immortal words of James T. Kirk, "I was out of control and blind as a bat."

Three thousand, seven hundred, and one miles later, I crossed the Ross Island Bridge. From there I made my way to Beaverton and checked into the Shilo Inn on Canyon Road. I chose Beaverton because it was on the outskirts of Portland but close enough to Tigard to visit one of the most iconic fly shops on the planet: Kaufmann's Streamborn. If anybody could point me in the right direction, it would be Kaufmann's.

For the last four or five years, I had devoured everything I could find that had anything to do with catching a steelhead. From what I could deduce, steelhead fishing was not that difficult. Little did I know at the time that that conclusion was either a juicy rationalization or a figment of my youthful imagination. Fishing for steelhead is essentially about spending time on the water and learning the nuances of a particular watershed. At some point you have to learn to read the water, wade, and make the cast, then hook and land the fish. The most aggravating thing about the sport is trying to wade through all the local jargon. It's almost as aggravating as translating ancient Chinese poetry from the Song Dynasty into something an average person might find interesting.

Portland was a beautiful city in the early 1970s. The city was experiencing a cultural renaissance of sorts. In some ways it represented the second coming of the Beat generation—not precisely the same, but close enough to attract a handful of poets and writers from San Francisco who would later influence a new generation of scribes. Years later, you could find them scattered throughout the small towns that dot the Oregon coast. Portland was not exactly what you might call conducive or inspirational for poetry and prose, but the coast, on the other hand, was dripping in inspiration, like the sap oozing out of the enormous coastal pines that lined the once-legendary steelhead rivers of the Oregon coast. Years later, the small towns along the coast grew famous for their mom-and-pop bookstores, local writers, and the arts and crafts festivals throughout the summer and fall.

Oregon was also home to every known pseudoscience imaginable. It was difficult to get away from all the bloodsucking leeches. The streets were bustling with faithful members of the local Hare Krishna movement begging for money. Members of the Church of Scientology were standing on every corner searching high and low for runaways or people who just wanted to go west for some reason or the other and didn't have anyplace to stay. They were ripe for the picking, especially the runaways. The city bus station was ground zero. The parasites lined up three deep at times. In the early 1970s, Portland would lead the nation in homeless children and runaways. The cults kept growing, and the kids kept coming, and no one seemed to know what to do with them.

It didn't take a genius to figure out I needed to find a job and a permanent place to live, quickly. I was spending way too much time at Kaufmann's. I was hoping someone there would offer me a job. I can't think of a better way to learn the local fisheries' ins and outs than from a local fly shop. Unfortunately, I was just another name on a long list of people waiting for the same thing.

A few days later, I was having lunch in a little diner in downtown Portland. It was only several hundred yards down the street from the Church of Scientology, which would probably explain all the unusual people in the diner. Out of nowhere, a tall, well-dressed man sat down beside me at the counter. I didn't think much about it at the time. The diner was almost full, and the seat next to me was open, and what the hell did I care. I have no idea which one of us started the conversation, but one thing led to another, and for the next several hours, we sat there and talked about anything and everything but nothing significant. He seemed fascinated that I would jump in a truck and drive all the way to Oregon to fish for steelhead. His name was Kyle Olinger, and he was the general manager of Bill Olinger Lincoln-Mercury, which just happened to be a few blocks down the road from the Shilo where I was staying. You can't make this stuff up. He offered me a job selling cars. I laughed, but at the same time, I was somewhat interested. After all, I did need a job.

The next day I met Kyle at the dealership and completed all the hire paperwork. The only obstacle I could see was that I only owned one pair of slacks, one dress shirt, and one pair of spiffy loafers. Finally, I told Kyle, "Thanks so much for the offer, but I just don't see how I can make this work."

The next thing I knew, we were walking into Washington Square Mall. Not to make too big a deal about it, but Kyle bought me four or five pairs of slacks, shirts to match, two dress jackets, and a new pair of shoes. When we returned to the dealership, he handed me the key to a new Monarch. Evidently, this was my new demo (even though, I have to admit, I didn't have a clue what a demo was). Then he handed me his business card and pointed to a new apartment complex down the road, and told me that if I had any problems to have the manager call him.

It was a strange set of events. Looking back, I kept thinking there had to be an ulterior motive behind Kyle's kindness. The next day I moved into a new apartment. Friday morning at eight o'clock I showed up for my first sales meeting. I was wearing a new suit and tie. I had a notebook in one hand and a fresh cup of coffee in the other. Kyle started laughing. He told me, "You don't look like a rookie. Whatever you do, don't let these idiots give you a hard time. Most of them are jerks."

By the time I arrived, the automobile industry was just coming out of the doldrums caused by the gas embargo of 1972. Car sales were climbing, but the recurring gas shortages essentially changed the industry forever, or at least for the next thirty or forty years. Demand for big cars like the Lincoln Town Car was almost nonexistent. The smaller four- and six-cylinder cars were on fire. I made more money the first month than I had made working an entire year for my stepfather. I was what they called a liner. I would meet and greet the customers, shake their hands, take them to the type of car they were interested in, and then excuse myself. I would turn and tell the potential customer, "Excuse me, I just started here this week, and I don't know much about the car business. Let me get you a real car salesman. Someone that knows what they're doing."

Then I would turn and walk away and not look back. I would find one of the better salesmen and bring him back to the customers, and per my script, I would say, "Mr. and Mrs. Suzy Cream Cheese, let me introduce you to Bud Dresser; he has been here for years. I'm more than sure he can find you the right car at the right price."

Then Bud would step in and sell them the car, and for that, I would get half the commission. On a good day, I could have four or five salesmen working for me, sometimes at the same time. I made enough money the first month to almost furnish my new apartment. My first piece of furniture was a full-wave waterbed (a waterbed without any baffles). The next month I bought a new Kenwood stereo. Hey, it was 1974, and I was seventeen.

On the one hand, the salesmen loved me because I was young and full of energy, not to mention I was putting a tremendous amount of money in their pockets. Then again, I was taking half their commission for little more than a handshake and a smile. No one knew exactly how to solve the dilemma, or even if they wanted to. Little did they know at the time, but I kept notes, and every day, my spiel was getting better. I had no idea how long this would last, but there must have been fifteen or twenty car dealerships in Beaverton and ten times that many in Portland and the surrounding suburbs. Salesmen seemed to come and go like the tides.

I was always bugging the other salesmen about the local fishing, and finally, Buddy Garry, one of the few salesmen who took the time to educate me on the fine arts of the sale, introduced me to John Nuttle, if for nothing else, to shut me up. It seems the local nightclubs, strip joints, and cardrooms were more conducive to a salesman's lifestyle than the local fisheries. The first time I met John, I was a little taken aback. I had seen him around the dealership many times and at the sales meetings, of course, but I don't remember seeing him on the lot chasing customers like the other salesmen. He spent the majority of his time in his office on the phone. John was in the neighborhood of six feet five and somewhere in the three-hundred-pound range. Later I found out he was an offensive lineman and an All-American at the University of Arizona. The Cincinnati Bengals drafted him in the early seventies, and unfortunately, he blew out his knee in spring training and was sent packing several months later.

The first thing I noticed about John was he had a tremendous appetite. God help you if you got between him and his food. The first time we went out to breakfast, he ordered a large stack of pancakes, a side order of bacon, another side order of sausage, and finally, topped it off with a huge slice of apple pie. The next thing I noticed about John was his proclivity to run his fingers through what little hair he left and then rub his nose when he realized he just screwed the pooch.

We spent the next several hours discussing the local steelhead fishing and an excessive amount of time talking about pro football. I was a huge Miami Dolphin fan at the time. Of course, it wasn't difficult to carry on a conversation about the Fins considering Miami had been in the last three Super Bowls and just happened to win the previous two. John was the kind of guy who was always telling jokes that no one seemed to understand. He was one of the most passive people on the planet; he never seemed to get angry with anyone. And if he did, he never stayed mad very long.

In some ways, he was the perfect fishing partner. He was off on Tuesdays and Thursdays, and he usually went fishing. The problem was that John primarily fished with conventional gear. Even though I didn't mind using traditional fishing gear, I wanted to catch a steelhead using a fly rod. I had no idea how this was going to work. To do my thing, I needed running water and the occasional pool with a decent tailout. It didn't seem to faze John in the least. He kept telling me about the Sandy River, and how, at the right time of year, the steelhead fishing was just about as good as it can get considering it was only a short drive from Portland. I didn't know if that sounded depressing or promising. It's been my experience that fisheries close to a significant city usually suck. Not necessarily the fishing as much as the fishing pressure, which is essentially the same thing.

When I finally had the chance to look at a map, I noticed that the Sandy was a tributary of the Columbia River. For some reason, I thought the coastal rivers and streams would be much more productive, especially for winter steelhead, and they were relatively close as the crow flies. It never occurred to me that Pacific salmon and steelhead migrated up the Columbia as far as the Snake and Salmon Rivers in Idaho. John and I planned to hit the Sandy the following Thursday morning. It gave me five days to find a decent pair of waders and boots.

Later that week John introduced me to G.I. Joe's. I didn't know it at the time, but I was looking at the future, essentially the end of the mom-and-pop fly shops. G.I. Joe's was the quintessential box store that carried everything for the modern outdoorsman. It was the West Coast version of L.L.Bean. I bought a pair of neoprene waders and wading boots, and later that day I stopped by Kaufmann's and loaded up on flies and tippet material and a few other odds and ends like thermal underwear and a "waterproof" jacket, a fishing license, and as much advice as I could garner from the boys. When I mentioned that I planned on fishing the Sandy Thursday morning, Randle didn't seem surprised. He asked me if I knew what section of the river we were going to fish, but sadly I didn't have a clue where John intended to fish. Randle mentioned, "The Sandy was fishing well, but the water may be a little high. It's been raining hard off and on the last several days, but you still have a few days for the river to drop. If it doesn't drop, the Sandy is not worth the time and energy."

I had exponentially more questions than they had answers. I stayed up late Wednesday night, rigging my Ted Williams saltwater fly rod, putting new fly line on my Shakespeare fly reel, and tying a half dozen new leaders. That's the problem with fly shops; if you ask for their advice, you're almost obligated to buy something.

I woke up early, took a shower, loaded my gear into the Bronco, grabbed a cup of coffee, and hit the road. John had asked me to meet him at seven that morning in the G.I. Joe's parking lot. John didn't show up, and after what seemed like a half hour or so, I had to find a pay phone and call him. He was still half asleep when he finally answered the phone.

I wanted to read him the riot act, but I didn't have the heart to complain. After all, he was taking me fishing. He made up some feeble excuse and promised he would be there posthaste. The problem was John lived on the other side of Portland, and assuming he already had his fishing gear packed, under the best of conditions it still would take him an hour to make it to the G.I. Joe's parking lot. And he had to navigate the morning traffic. I called him back and suggested we meet at Carrows Restaurant on Canyon Road. That way, I could have a leisurely breakfast and read the *Oregonian*, the local newspaper. If nothing else, I could peruse the local fishing reports.

By the time John managed to drag his sorry derriere into Carrows, I had already finished breakfast and devoured most of the *Oregonian*. I had finished off an entire pot of coffee and managed to work myself into a tither. I was past the point of caring. When John finally made his way to the table, I stood up, grabbed the check, and was about to pay the bill and make my way to the Bronco when John sheepishly asked, "Do we have time for breakfast?"

By this time, it was almost nine o'clock, and for all practical purposes, what difference did it make, so I sighed, "Sure, knock yourself out. It's only nine o'clock. We have all day."

Somewhere in the background, a busboy slipped and dropped a bus lug full of dishes in between two tables. It sounded like the proverbial runaway bull in a china shop. John kept asking, "What did you say? I can't hear you over all the noise."

I said, "Sure, knock yourself out."

I looked around; by this time, the restaurant was almost full. There was no telling how long it would take John to get his food and finish his meal. I was beginning to wonder if this was still a good idea. Sometimes it's better to throw in the towel and call it a day. John seemed oblivious to the time. At this point, I would have considered it a minor victory just to see the damn Sandy. When his food finally arrived, he wolfed it down, then grabbed my check, paid both bills, and made his way through the crowd like a pulling guard looking for an outside linebacker to block. For a big man, he was light on his feet. It wasn't difficult to see what the Bengals liked about John when they first scouted him at the University of Arizona. I jumped into the Bronco, expecting him to throw his gear in the back of my truck and pile in, but he jumped in his demo and told me to follow him. Like everything else that morning, it didn't make much sense, but I did it anyway.

A few minutes later, we pulled into the G.I. Joe's parking lot. At first I thought we would load my Bronco and get the hell out of here, but no, John needed to pick up a few things. I was about to get introduced to the thousands of various plastic baits, spin and glows, spoons, spinners, and multitude of plugs that were explicitly designed for steelhead, not to mention live sand shrimp and cured salmon eggs. Of course, John had to work his way up and down every aisle and explain the nuances of all the techniques created throughout the years to catch a steelhead. At some level, it made fly fishing seem rather dull.

About this time, I was ready to get down on my hands and knees and beg John to stop the insanity. Let's go fishing. I was beginning to think this was just a cruel joke. But he walked out of G.I. Joe's with several hundred dollars' worth of junk. He transferred three rods and a pair of boots and several jackets into the Bronco, locked up his demo, and then dumped two bags of God only knows what into my back seat. Finally, we were headed in the direction of the Sandy River; it was a small victory, but a victory nonetheless.

Fifteen minutes later, I pulled into a coffee shop and picked up a couple of cups of java and an assortment of doughnuts while John stayed in the truck. When I finally climbed into the Bronco, John seemed aggravated. Then he started to give me a ration of cow manure about taking so long. Finally, he looked at me and barked, "If you keep stopping every ten minutes, we are never going to get to the Sandy, much less catch any fish. By the way, did you pick up cream and sugar?"

It was everything I could do not to pull over and leave his sorry ass on the side of the road. I had to bite my tongue, and a few minutes later, I replied, "You do know it's ten-thirty, and we were supposed to be on the water and fishing by eight o'clock this morning. Yet you want to give me a ration of crap for stopping for a cup of coffee."

The day was starting to look like a Laurel and Hardy movie. It was a walking, talking clusterf***, and yes, reality can be stranger than fiction, especially when it came to John. Eventually, we made it to the Sandy River. Up until that point, I thought John knew the river well enough to know exactly where he wanted to fish. I was wrong on so many levels.

The river was running several feet over the banks, and even though you could see it was a beautiful river, I didn't see anywhere we could fish, much less wade. We started working our way up the river, hoping to find a more suitable place to fish. Then we started working our way down the river, as if the lower river would be in better shape.

For the next several hours, faced with a river that was for all practical purposes unfishable, we did what most despondent fishermen do: We kept hoping, praying, and begging the sun to come out and the river to miraculously drop. Then John suggested the Clackamas River. The Clackamas was even closer to town. By this time, it was drizzling again, not quite raining but enough to puddle up the pullouts. (Of course, it had been drizzling since the day I arrived.)

For the life of me, I will never understand why John thought the Clackamas would be in any better shape than the Sandy. As far as I was concerned, the day was a flop, but I didn't have anything else better to do and, for the most part, John was good company. If nothing else, now I knew where the Sandy River was. According to John, the Clackamas fished better than the Sandy in the fall. One could only ask then, why did we waste time on the Sandy when we could have gone directly to the Clackamas? It had something to do with summer-run fish versus winter-run fish. Some of the rivers had a good run of summer fish and, for some reason, didn't necessarily get a run of winter fish and vice versa. Some of the rivers were lucky enough to have summer and winter runs. But I just scratched my head and thought, what the hell does it matter at this point?

Believe it or not, the Clackamas *was* in better shape than the Sandy. Even though the water was still high, the river was exponentially cleaner. Later that day, we bumped into a few drift boats dredging some of the deeper pools. It seemed like everyone we stopped and talked to seemed to be using conventional gear and cured salmon eggs or some kind of plastic thingamajig. What made the Clackamas so appealing was the access. For the most part, a two-lane road followed the river as it meandered through the small canyons. All you had to do was find a place to pull off the road and park.

We finally found a good run that actually had plenty of parking and easy access to the river. Pullouts can be interesting in so many ways; certainly they can be busy at times, but then again, they provide easy access to the river. One assumes a pullout is empty because that section of the river doesn't fish very well. The first thing I noticed about rivers is no one actually fishes the pullouts. And yet any access to the river is to be appreciated; if nothing else, it gets you in the water and actually fishing (which happens to be the only way I know to actually hook and land a fish). Pullout or not, this was where I was going to plant my flag, and if John didn't want to fish here, then he could sit in the Bronco and eat doughnuts and drink cold coffee.

This was also the first time I ever tried to put on a pair of neoprene waders and boots. Personally, it was a miserable experience and rather embarrassing. It must have taken twenty minutes or so to climb into my waders and another twenty minutes to slide my boots on. By the time I finally managed to tie the boots I noticed I was soaking wet. Between the rain and the perspiration, I was drenched. I grabbed my rod and my official fly-fishing vest and headed down to the river. I worked my way down current looking for what I considered a good stretch of the river to fish. Then again, what the hell did I really know?

About sixty or seventy yards downriver, I found what I thought was a good-looking stretch of water. About thirty feet from the bank, I noticed a huge boulder just underneath the surface of the water. The water was sliding over the top of the boulder, and on each side there seemed to be two deep channels. Up until this point, I had never waded a river with any significant current, but I had seen this scenario in a multitude of fly-fishing books, especially the ones that concentrated on steelhead.

I was lucky there was nothing behind me but some tall grass. I stripped off forty or fifty feet of line and made a reasonably good cast. The fly landed ten, maybe twelve feet up current of the boulder. I let the fly swing down current, and as it passed the boulder something grabbed my fly and turned downstream. Several minutes later I heard John rustling through the woods. By the time he arrived, I was sitting on my ass with my legs spread in about six inches of water with a nice six- or seven-pound steelhead between them. I'll admit it wasn't necessarily a big one, but it was a steelhead nonetheless. Then I heard John say, "I told you I would put you on a steelhead."

It took me two years to hook and land another steelhead on the fly.

You Can't Always Get What You Want

ALEXANDER POPE, IN HIS FAMOUS ESSAY CALLED "AN ESSAY ON MAN," wrote, "Hope springs eternal in the human breast."

Sure, hope springs eternal in the human breast, but a good plan and a little luck don't hurt either. Twelve years ago, I hatched a plan that might put me in a position to catch my first Atlantic salmon. It was fraught with land mines and more ifs, ands, and buts than you could imagine. First, I needed to reach out and find an Atlantic salmon lodge gullible enough to agree to my offer. Then I needed to convince my close friend the world-class photographer Mark Lance to come along. Normally that wouldn't be a problem, but at the mere mention of Atlantic salmon, Mark takes a deep breath and rolls his eyes. That should have been the first clue.

Connecting with a lodge owner or a guide during high season is always an adventure. After weeks of trying, I had almost given up hope of reaching Jack Barlow, the general manager and head guide at Camp Brule on the Little Cascapédia in Quebec, and with it my cunning scheme to finagle my way into my first trip fly-fishing for Atlantic salmon. A few days after a last-ditch effort, leaving my umpteenth message, lightning struck, and Jack and I both ended up on the line simultaneously. I introduced myself as the publisher and managing editor of *The Contemporary Sportsman* and *The Contemporary Wing Shooter*. I started to explain my situation when I heard Jack bark orders about the importance of keeping the fly in the water and fishing out the swing.

It sounded familiar but somewhat off topic, then it dawned on me that Jack was calling from the boat. Indeed, Jack soon apologized and explained that he was on the water with a client. Since Jack assured me that his client was not offended by our conversation, I did my best to work around their ongoing discourse. Trying for maximum professionalism, I worked on tempering my excitement as I explained that I wanted to bring a photographer up and spend the week chasing Atlantic salmon on the Little Cascapédia to write an article about the experience and then publish it in *The Contemporary Sportsman*.

Jack asked the name of the photographer, and before I had time to tell him I hadn't decided yet, he blurted out that he had in his possession dozens of photos taken by Mark Lance several years prior. I was afraid that might come up: I had known about the photos long before I called—they were parked on a CD on top of my desk. As I had feared, Jack volunteered to write the article in my stead, sprinkled with Mark's preexisting photos. I had to change the parameters of the argument on the fly, no pun intended, sensing my clever scheme for scoping out a new lodge and concomitantly finagling my way into Camp Brule for a week of salmon fishing slipping away. I explained that the article was meant to be about *my* first Atlantic salmon on the fly. Perhaps seeing through my cunning designs, Jack started to laugh and capitulated, but informed me that he didn't have any openings until the season was over. He thought the fishing might be better in the fall anyway, so we settled on the first week of September. Granted, most experts might not consider fall prime time, but if we were lucky, if the late-season rains showed and the proverbial creek didn't rise too much, I might catch my first Atlantic salmon after all.

Inviting myself to Camp Brule turned out to be the easy part. The real challenge involved explaining to my wife why I had just tacked another ten days onto my already two-week-long trip covering lodges on the Skeena and the Buckley Rivers in British Columbia. While I was at it, I also intended to spend another three days camping on the Rapid River and chasing landlocked salmon at the mouth of the Mooselookmeguntic.

Mark Lance, my partner in crime for the Camp Brule trip, flew in from Denver a few days early so we could take our time meandering up and down the Gaspé Peninsula, as was our modus operandi on most road trips, even the 16,000-mile road trips. When Mark finally arrived, a few hours late, he had that beaten-down look we all acquire after a long flight. I offered to take him to his room so he could unpack and take a shower before dinner, but he wouldn't hear of it. It wasn't difficult to see that Mark needed a cold beer and some real food.

Later that evening, we dragged Mark's luggage up to his hotel room and agreed to meet before daybreak the next morning in the lobby. Mark was once a geologist by trade, and like all scientists, he gets kind of testy about schedules. So I set my alarm clock for four o'clock in the morning and made sure to be showered, packed, and stowed by the time Mark came down the elevator.

When we met up that morning, we exchanged a discerning smile, each of us knowing he was thinking exactly what the other was thinking: pancakes with fresh maple syrup, and bacon. Ten minutes later, we were headed north, looking for a mom-and-pop diner. After all, this was Maine, home of some of the best maple syrup on the planet. We found our diner, collected fuel for the long trek, and enjoyed the first leg of our trip well before putting a line in the water.

September in the north embodies the beginning of the end: a time of transition. In due course, the Gaspé would be smothered in snow, but for now, it was the time of the harvest moon and the season of abundance for farmers and hunters. Several weeks earlier, I had been sloshing my way through the rain forest of British Columbia, chasing steelhead. I didn't remember how much I missed fall in the north woods until the sun started rising over the timbers of northern Maine, beginning to show their fall colors. When we hit the New Brunswick border, the woods were ablaze in intense reds, bumblebee yellows, and mango browns—the complete opposite of the monochromatic green, longleaf wiregrass forest of my sweet home in southern Alabama.

Travel, to me, is about celebrating the differences: not only the difference in the landscape, climate, and biodiversity but also the difference in the people and cultural diversity. There is nothing better than a long, slow road trip to understand the relationship between people and the landscape, especially the people who make their living off the land. It is comforting that there are still people who live their lives in harmony with the natural world.

Making good time, we pulled into the lodge a day early. We figured if the camp was full, we could find a hotel and crash for the night. But to my surprise, Camp Brule was empty—never a good omen. If the fishing is as good in the fall as advertised during Jack's sales pitch for this particular week in September, why were we the only ones here? Jack walked out of his office to greet us, and even before we had completed our pleasantries, I asked where everybody was. Although he greeted Mark quite warmly, his reception of me, following my awkward question, teetered somewhat on the chilly side. Ignoring my inquiry, Jack invited us in for a cup of coffee. I asked again why the lodge was empty. He took a deep breath and lectured me like a small child that the water was low and the temperature currently more suitable for bonefish than Atlantic salmon. From there, his remarks turned to the advantages of having the lodge to ourselves. I saw my chances for catching my first Atlantic salmon on a fly wane.

For its part, Camp Brule lived up to everything I had imagined: a beautiful old lodge exuding old-world charm, sitting in a gorgeous place, with a world-class Atlantic salmon river right out the back door. Convenient for the novice salmon fly fisherman, it's one of those places where you could spend a week and never fret if you didn't catch that elusive salmon.

After unpacking and scoping out the lodge, Mark wanted to take a few photos in the late-afternoon light. With beginner's enthusiasm, I strung up a few rods, put on my waders, and stretched out the lines in the pool behind the lodge while Mark used me as his model. To our utter astonishment, the photo shoot only lasted a short while before Jack came running down the steps screaming at me to get out of the water. Apparently, for some reason, Camp Brule doesn't own the pool behind the lodge; it's owned by a lodge on the Grand Cascapédia. For the life of me, I don't remember the name of that lodge, possibly because its mere mention seemed to aggravate Jack. The entangled and confusing rules of access to local waters form part of the cultural charm of the Gaspé. I suspect it's also one massive insider joke to identify and haze first-time tourists.

Mark and I spent the next five days floating the Little Cascapédia. On Mark's previous trip to Camp Brule, he had caught his one and only Atlantic salmon: a beautiful eighteen-pound hen. He liked to tell me about it in great detail when, during the next seven days, no salmon even sniffed my fly. In fact, I didn't see an Atlantic salmon until we decided to hike into the Bonaventure.

We arrived late at the Bonaventure River to find a gaggle of fishermen in what should have been our pool. The sight of six or seven fishermen lined up, waiting their turn to fish the pool, admittedly dampened our spirits at first. Our guide didn't seem to worry much about the infringement of our rights. He did his best to explain the funky rules and regulations that control the Bonaventure and some of the other local rivers: something about the ZEC, the Cascapedia River Society, and the lottery. To the uninitiated, it all sounded a bit complicated (not to mention expensive). More to the point, my overriding motivation was catching an Atlantic salmon, not passing the Canadian bar. For one ill-tempered moment, I looked at Mark and asked, "Really, we drove two thousand miles each way to do this?" From the lofty height of having already caught his one (and only) Atlantic salmon, Mark again reminded me that he had warned me of the slim odds of catching an Atlantic salmon on my first trip. Mark had done his best to prepare me for failure. When that didn't curb my occasional impatient grumbling, he reminded me that I was the one who invited him.

The day following our shoulder-to-shoulder adventure on the Bonaventure, Jack managed to garner us a "great" pool on the Grand Cascapédia. He dropped us off at the Cascapedia River Society early the following morning. From what I could make out, he had paid the Society $1800 for the day. That got us an Atlantic salmon canoe, an ancient guide, and a young man to do the dirty work. When the gear was packed and the sports safely aboard, the ancient mariner gingerly strutted down the rocks, climbed in the canoe, and grabbed the push pole.

For the next four hours, we fished our way down the pool and then switched flies and repeated the process until it was lunchtime. The pool was only forty or fifty yards long, and regardless of how slowly you fished it, you were continually starting over. Like Oliver Twist, the boy who dared to ask for more porridge, I had the gall to ask our guide why we couldn't fish the pools below us. Then I topped off that affront by suggesting we float the river until we found a good stretch of water, anchor the canoe, and get out and fish it. Once I had managed to finally revive our seasoned and venerable guide, I feared he was going to beat me over the head with the push pole. For some odd reason, he kept asking where I was from—apparently it makes a difference.

Some years following my first trip to the Grand Cascapédia, I fished with a local Mi'gmaq guide, and he told me about his tribe and about the tribe's fishing rights on the Grand Cascapédia. From what I could tell, it was incredibly complicated, but ensured that the Mi'gmaq tribe received its fair compensation for the use of its rivers, which explained some of the quirks that had struck me as a bit unusual on my first visit. Another thing I took away from the conversation was that the guide is king. If a guide wanted to pitch a stick of dynamite into the best pool on the river, no one could stop him. Then again, a guide conveyed this information to me, and some guides don't necessarily let the constraints of truth get in the way of a good tale.

Later that day, Jack picked us up and took us back to the lodge for the big meal of the day and an afternoon nap. After what seemed like a rather long nap, we were back on the river and repeated the morning ritual for several more hours, unfortunately with the same results. That night we enjoyed a great dinner and cocktails before crawling into a cozy bed.

All in all, we spent seven days on the Little and the Grand Cascapédia on my first visit. Although I didn't get so much as a rise, I knew better than to rush to judgment about Atlantic salmon fishing. After all, Mark had warned me. Plus, it wasn't the first time I've come up empty-handed, and I doubt it will be the last.

The Gaspé in the fall is downright breathtaking; it's not difficult to see the hand of some divine power in the beauty of the rivers and valleys we floated. It some ways, it is a spiritual experience, a quest of sorts. Is Atlantic salmon fishing for everyone? No, it's most certainly not! Is it for me? Absolutely! It appeals to everything I love about fishing: the hunt, the challenge, the people, the rivers, the land, and the travel. It's not necessarily what you take from the river. It's about what you give back. If you happen to be the privileged fisherman who on any given day catches an Atlantic salmon, count yourself as one of the luckiest people on the planet and brag about it mercilessly to those who haven't yet. It's a sacred part of the tradition.

All great road trips eventually come to an end. I dropped Mark off at the airport in Portland, Maine, and then pointed the Suburban south. I drove straight through, only stopping for gas and the occasional burger. At the end of this trip, I hadn't seen my family in almost four weeks; I missed them and hoped my wife hadn't changed the locks and sold all my fishing gear to the lowest bidder. She hadn't, and coming home to my loving family always ranks high as the final joy associated with a great fishing trip, regardless if you catch a damn Atlantic salmon or not.

Fortune Always Favors the Foolish

BARELY ACROSS THE CONNECTICUT BORDER, MY CELL PHONE STARTED ringing. I didn't recognize the number at first, but for some reason, it reminded me of a Canadian area code. Why shouldn't it—I had been in Canada for the last four weeks. I was beginning to think, act, and occasionally speak like a Canadian guide, which is scary on so many levels. At first, I thought it was Jack at Camp Brule. I couldn't think of one good reason he might be calling unless I forgot something at the lodge, or I absconded with the family jewels. It wasn't that I was opposed to answering the phone, but the highway was littered with signs warning drivers that it was against the law to talk on your cell phone and drive at the same time. It was something about the five-hundred-dollar fine that made me a little reluctant, so I let the call go to voice mail.

A few hours later, I pulled into a Waffle House for a quick bite. Usually I never stop and piss my money away at a chain restaurant, although they have their advantages. If you order a cheeseburger at a McDonald's in Maine, it probably tastes like a cheeseburger at any McDonald's in South Florida. Joe Hovious and I have been known to drive fifty or sixty miles out of our way to run down a good mom-and-pop restaurant, especially if it's a diner, and spend hours trying to find it again on the way back. When possible, Mark and I do our best to stay off the interstate, usually running into them accidentally. That's the cost of admission if you're traveling with a professional photographer. (I would be more inclined to call Mark an artist, even though he would scoff at the idea.) Of course, it's a fallacy to think that all mom-and-pop restaurants are created equal. Like all things in life, it's a crapshoot. Rarely can you find one on a major highway, and if you do, the food is usually mediocre at best. If it was indeed a great mom-and-pop restaurant, you would have to wait in line or hope you could find a couple of empty seats at the counter. Unfortunately, this time the quest would have to wait. As the Bandit might say, I was "southbound and down, loaded up and truckin.'" It was time to go home. At this point, I had been north of the Mason-Dixon Line way too long.

About halfway through my All-Star Special, I remembered I had several messages on my phone. It wasn't Jack or Mark. It was the lodge owner that must not be named. From this point on, I will call the lodge owner Voldemort for lack of a more appropriate name, and the lodge Hogwarts. Voldemort wanted to know if I was interested in visiting his lodge on the Matapédia River next season. He wanted me to bring a photographer up to shoot photos for his new website. We would get seven days guided fishing, and room and board, for the images. It seemed almost too good to be true, if the Matapédia was still a reasonably good salmon river.

The Matapédia essentially straddles the border between Quebec and New Brunswick. From what I knew about the Matapédia (which wasn't very much), it was at one time considered one of the best, if not the best, Atlantic salmon river in Quebec. Of course, at one time all the rivers that ran to the sea throughout eastern Canada were considered cosmic. But the only way to find out was to fish the damn thing.

There always seems to be a quid pro quo involved in these offers. There was still the cosmic catch, the universal truth, and a carrot-on-the-end-of-a-stick sales pitch. John Nash would have been proud to know that every modern-day lodge owner is well versed in the Nash Equilibrium. The mathematical formula is a proposed solution of a non-cooperative game theory involving two or more players, principally with both players benefiting equally in the spoils. Typically, when someone offers me the deal of a lifetime, Nash Equilibrium or not, I run for the hills. Regardless of what someone tells you, there is no such thing as a free trip. Even the most basic free trip these days will set you back several thousand dollars.

At that point, I don't think I could have suffered through another seven days without hooking and landing a salmon, although it's not uncommon not to catch a salmon. In fact, it seems to be the norm, not the exception. It's the nature of the game we pay to play. Sometimes I think it's much better to approach these trips with a more holistic perspective. If you consistently try to break down the journey into smaller parts, you will drive yourself crazy. Suppose you decide to justify the trip by dividing the trip's cost by the number of salmon you catch. In that case, you will find yourself on your knees with a very sharp samurai sword about to commit seppuku, the samurai's traditional way to redeem himself to the local warlord and restore his honor. I can think of less painful ways, like putting in more time on the water, learning how to cast better, and learning to read the water—and if that fails, try golf. The idea of splitting my stomach open with a razor-sharp sword and then watching my guts spill out on the ground is a little melodramatic. In the end, it's just fishing, for Christ's sake.

We agreed to keep in touch, and after I was home for a few weeks, I would give him a call back and discuss the trip in more depth. Somewhere in southern Kentucky, I managed to reach Mark and fill him in on Voldemort's proposal, if for nothing else to see if he was even interested. I wouldn't say he seemed thrilled, but then again, it was another chance to catch an Atlantic salmon, and it's been my impression that fortune always favors the foolish. The more I thought about it, I probably should have waited a few months before I called Mark. He had just stepped off the horse, and I wasn't sure his heart was in it.

I was in striking distance of Mobile. With a little luck, I could be home before nightfall. After a few days of unpacking, catching up on random chores, and spoiling my wife, I had to get back to work. The summer was ending, and fall was right around the corner. To make things a little more aggravating for my wife, I was headed back to British Columbia the last week of October and first week of November to chase steelhead.

In January, I was headed to southern Oregon to chase winter steelhead. In May, June, and July, I would be fishing the beaches of Sanibel and Captiva for snook and tarpon. But the Matapédia seemed intriguing. Of course, it involved another long road trip. Then, out of the blue, I received a phone call from Neville Orsmond, the relatively new owner of Thomas & Thomas fly rods. He wanted to advertise in *The Contemporary*

Sportsman, and if I had time, could I stop by and shoot the photography for T&T's new catalog? At first, "stopping by" sounded a little ridiculous; you do not just "stop by" when you live at opposite end of the country. Then it dawned on me: T&T was in western Massachusetts, and if Mark and I flew into Boston and rented an SUV at the airport, we could drive west and spend three or four days at T&T, and then head northeast toward the Matapédia, killing two birds with one stone. The T&T job was an easy sell, but back-to-back trips might be difficult for Mark to justify. Even though July seemed like a long way off, I knew from experience that it was right around the corner. It's not like we had to start packing tomorrow, but we needed to stay on top of it.

The fall and spring vaporized, and suddenly it was late May and I was on Sanibel chasing snook on the beach. I barely had time to get back to Mobile and start packing for the Gaspé. Even though the Matapédia River might not exactly be on the Gaspé, it's definitely close enough for government work. It was a strange dichotomy—the ninety-degree temperatures and white-sand beaches of Sanibel and the cooler and almost fall-like temperatures and green forest of northern Canada.

A few weeks later, I was about to land in Boston, a city I had promised my wife I would never set foot in again. After grad school, my wife took a job at Vertex Pharmaceuticals in Cambridge. We lasted three or four years, and even though my wife dearly loved her career, she understood that I had to get out of the damn Northeast Corridor or I was going to commit hara-kiri sooner rather than later. I had already picked up the rental car when Mark finally landed. By the time we made it to the Suburban, it was almost five o'clock, and the afternoon traffic was already stacked up at the tollbooths. I tried my best to explain to Mark what we were in for the next several hours, but I got the feeling he thought I was exaggerating. Little did he know at the time, I was trying to shine a positive light on the nightmare ahead.

We headed west at a snail's pace. Mark was fortunate that I had spent three years driving in this ridiculous traffic. In Boston's defense, my wife and I lived there during the Big Dig's high-water mark. I remember the day we left like it was yesterday. When we finally crossed the Mason-Dixon Line, I pulled the moving truck off the road and got out and kissed the ground. I swore to myself I would never cross that line again. Of course, I forgot that all the great Atlantic salmon and steelhead rivers lived north of the Mason-Dixon Line.

By the time we made it to western Massachusetts, the sun was starting to fade. We were both exhausted! I was coming down with the flu. Either that or Mark already had the flu. When I harken back to the crime in question, I think Mark showed up at the airport with the flu and shook my hand or gave me a bear hug. Regardless of how it started, I spent the next several days in bed while Mark started shooting the photography for T&T's new catalog. I did manage to spend some time in T&T's facility. The shop was nothing like I expected. It was an old-world shop littered with artifacts from a time gone by, a more genteel time when craftsmanship was more important than mass production. Everything smelled of history and bamboo and resin. The next morning, we did our best to hit the road early, but unfortunately, we couldn't leave town without stopping at all the coffee shops and the occasional bagel shop on the way out.

Later that day, we found ourselves just shy of the Canadian border. It was getting late, and we knew we had to find a motel quickly or we would be sleeping in the truck. We knew once we crossed the border, there was a cluster of motels about two hours down the highway. It was about nine o'clock when we pulled into the parking lot of the same motel we had stayed in the previous year. We might have reached the motel a little quicker if we could have ignored the multitudes of Tim Hortons along the way. That's how we measure the distance to the Gaspé: the number of Tim Hortons per mile. The motel wasn't exactly the Ritz-Carlton by any stretch of the imagination, but we did have a bed and a reasonably hot shower. Both of us were coughing and hacking and a little stuffed up—not exactly at our best.

Voldemort suggested we arrive at the lodge sometime around lunchtime. If not, we would have to find something to do until dinnertime. Evidently the lodge was closed while he was on the water guiding. Did I mention Mark and I never went anywhere fast? We were perpetually late for everything. We pulled into the lodge a little after one o'clock; true to his word Voldemort was back on the water, and the lodge was locked up like a supermax prison.

Mark and I headed toward the little town of Causapscal, where the Salmon River meets the Matapédia. We stumbled into a great small restaurant that hung out over the river and specialized in smoked meats and great pizzas. My God, what a combination! Before the week was over, we must have wolfed down a half dozen of them in every flavor imaginable. After lunch, we took the Atlantic salmon tour in the little public park across the street. To my surprise, it was beautiful and quite informative, and yes, it even had a few live salmon in the ponds. It occurred to me that if the fishing was as bad as last year on the Little Cascapédia, we could always sneak in one night and pilfer a few salmon. After all, how many times can one suffer the humiliation of getting skunked? I still had the open scars from the Little Cascapédia.

The little town of Routhierville was charming in an odd kind of way. If not for the beautiful old covered bridge on the Matapédia, I am not sure anyone would know the little town existed. We managed to waste the afternoon and started making our way back to Hogwarts. We must have stopped dozens of times to check out the pools on the river along the way. When we finally pulled in the long driveway, we spotted Voldemort trying to take a massive outboard off one of the largest Atlantic salmon canoes I have ever seen. I will spare you the details, but it wasn't a pretty picture. I wish it were something I could get out of my head!

To my surprise, Hogwarts was a beautiful little lodge. We loved everything about it, except the second floor. There were four bedrooms with two beds per room and only one shared bathroom for potentially eight people. Hogwarts doubled as a hybrid of sorts—a fishing lodge, a hotel, and sometimes a bed-and-breakfast. It was a little confusing at times, but if nothing else, it was entertaining. If you were the type of person who can't function in the morning without a shower, you had to crawl out of bed somewhere around four o'clock. The shower didn't seem to bother the other guests on the second floor, but it was directly above Voldemort's bedroom and woke him up every morning. The first morning I walked down the stairs as quietly as I could to find Voldemort pacing back in forth. He wanted to know what the hell I was doing. I politely asked what the hell difference did it make to him. That was the first morning, and it really didn't get much better. In fact, at the time, I thought that was the high point of the trip.

The food was excellent, though, and the lodge (other than the one bathroom) was very well laid out. Hogwarts was on a steep hill that overlooked the Matapédia. There were several small houses and an old church that had been converted into a small lodge. A gentleman who owned a fly shop somewhere in the states owned the homes, renting the rooms to his clientele from the fly shop. He wasn't supposed to guide and, to be honest, I never saw him guide anyone, but according to Voldemort, he was the second coming of the Antichrist. Voldemort had filed several lawsuits and did his best to have him evicted. To make things even worse, one of the best runs on the river was just below Hogwarts, and every morning at sunrise, three or four of the fishermen that were staying in the small houses were lined up shoulder to shoulder, taking turns swinging the bridge pool—arguably one of the best salmon pools on the river.

The first morning Mark and I decided to walk down to the river and check out the old converted church while Voldemort cleaned up the kitchen and took care of the other guests. Halfway down the road, we ran into a couple of spey fishermen from Scotland. Like all fishermen, we started asking all the obligatory who, what, when, and where questions all fishermen seem to ask on a strange river. If I remember correctly, they had caught a few salmon the previous week before the water started to drop. One of the gentlemen with a wee Scottish accent asked where we were staying. I pointed toward Hogwarts, and for the next few minutes, they started laughing uncontrollably. When they finally stopped, they asked if we were fishing with Voldemort, and for lack of a better answer, I told them the whole story, and they started laughing again. I was beginning to think that I should have owned a comedy club instead of a travel agency for fly fishermen. I halfway expected a tip after providing so much free entertainment. I never knew I was that funny!

Evidently, they had fished with Voldemort for a couple of days the previous week. The only thing we could get them to say was something about Voldemort losing his paddle or his push pole, falling asleep in the canoe, and slipping and sliding on the rocks while trying to get the canoe either on or off the trailer. There might have been something about falling out of the canoe, but I was already depressed by this time and didn't need to hear anymore. On the way back to the lodge, I reminded Mark that the Scots have a wicked sense of humor. If we were lucky, they were making it all up. A few years back, Mark and I ran into a couple of Scottish ghillies and their sport on the Skeena River in British Columbia over dinner. I laughed so hard throughout dinner I had a difficult time keeping anything down. Although I have to admit, I never really knew if they were pulling our leg or not. You never knew if they were kidding at our expense or deadpan serious.

The sun was beginning to rise over the valley walls, and there was still no sign of Voldemort. I thought we would have already landed several fish by now. After all, this is the Matapédia. After he finished cleaning up the kitchen and God only knows what else, Voldemort finally hooked up the canoe to his truck, and the first thing he said was would we mind using our SUV and running the shuttle? Usually, I wouldn't have given it a second thought, but it was the way he asked, and yes, by now, we were both a little apprehensive about the start of the first day (even though Mark is way too nice to ever admit it). By the end of the week, I thought Mark would probably drown him and possibly steal his canoe.

The Matapédia seems to have everything you would want from a world-class salmon river, except the world-class salmon. The river seemed to be in great shape. The water was clear, and overnight a few decent showers had cooled the river. It didn't take long to figure out that Voldemort was just going through the motions. The fishing was spectacular! It was the catching that left a lot to be desired. Mark spent the week taking photos of the landscape and the lodge and as many photos of the food as possible. He took photos of Voldemort and me getting in and out of the canoe. He took dozens of photos of all the wildflowers along the river. He took photos from the lodge looking down on the river, and then photos of the lodge looking up from the river.

Eventually, one afternoon I couldn't stand it anymore. I asked Voldemort how many fish he had caught this year. He turned, and in a small voice said, "None so far."

I wondered, how could this be? I had seen other fishermen up and down the river catch fish. The salmon had to be in the river, and yet we hadn't had so much as a tug. When we went back to the lodge for dinner that night, Mark was frustrated. He wanted to know how in the hell were we going to get any decent photos of an Atlantic salmon for Hogwarts? If nothing else, Voldemort could buy a few off the web and just lie about the fish's origin. Then I kept thinking about the salmon at the park. Maybe they would let us take a few photos of the salmon in the ponds. We had been doing the same thing day after day for the last six days without so much as a tug. If you counted the last seven days on the Little Cascapédia the previous year, we had been doing the same thing for thirteen days without touching a fish. And yes, I was counting! We had one day left, and we needed to catch a damn salmon. About this time, we were beginning to think we were cursed. I knew if Mark didn't catch a salmon on this trip, I would never be able to talk him into coming back. It was getting to be nothing more than a case of self-flagellation. I was beginning to enjoy the pain and humiliation of getting skunked day in and day out.

We were on the water early the next morning. Voldemort started high up on the river. He wanted to spend the whole day on the water and pull out below the lodge in Routhierville, just below the covered bridge. I had been fishing a single-handed rod with a ten-pound tippet almost the entire week. Like the previous six days, we floated and admired the scenery and took pictures of anything interesting. Seven agonizing hours later, we floated into the last pool before we had to pull out. Mark and I were arguing about whose turn it was to fish the bridge pool. Mark had pretty much given up and started breaking down his rod. I didn't have the heart to pick up the fly rod anymore, much less swing the last pool, regardless of how famous the bridge pool was. Mark kept pushing me to stand up and start casting.

By the time we reached the pool, Voldemort had pulled the canoe off to the river's starboard side so I could swing the deeper water off to the left. The river's right side was too shallow to fish, littered with rubble and the occasional large granite boulder, a stark reminder that this valley was carved by mammoth glaciers that once smothered most of North America at the end of the Pleistocene. From what I could tell, there was no appreciable reason to be that close to the bank. The canoe kept scraping the bottom and every few minutes would get stuck, and then Voldemort had to get his rather large caboose out of the canoe and push us back into the deeper water.

At times, it felt like I was a character in a Laurel and Hardy movie. Voldemort kept reminding me to fish left and stay away from the right side, explaining that there was nothing but grilse on the right side. Hell, a grilse sounded pretty good at this point. I kept pounding the left side like the obedient sport. I spotted a big flat rock off the canoe's starboard side about sixty or seventy yards from the pullout. It was pushing a lot of water, and there was a deep pool behind the rock. I asked Voldemort about the small, if not micro pool, and he kept telling me to ignore it. The small pool was only about ten feet from the canoe. I stripped in my line and was about to make another cast to the left, then instead decided to flip my fly line over my right shoulder and let the fly swing through the pool. Voldemort immediately started pitching a fit and screamed, "Cast left."

About that time, I finally got a hit! Voldemort began screaming, "Get it in the boat; it's just a grilse."

The rod doubled, and regardless of how much pressure I put on the fish, it never slowed down. The fish slowly swam away as if it didn't have a care in the world. By this time, it was thirty or forty feet downriver. Voldemort kept telling me to get the damn grilse to the boat. I can't tell you how bad I wanted Mark to slap the crap out of Voldemort. About that time, a rather large salmon jumped out of the water in the middle of the river with my fly in its mouth. When the salmon hit the water again, it took off with a vengeance, as if it had finally figured out something was wrong. It's almost as if the salmon had decided to flee rather than stand and fight. I am not saying that salmon have the cognitive ability to dwell on a predicament and make a choice, but then again, who really knows what goes on in the mind of an Atlantic salmon in these situations. Voldemort panicked and started yelling, "It's not a grilse, it's not a grilse. Back off on the damn drag or you're going to lose the fish."

I turned and said, "No shit, buckwheat."

Seconds later, Voldemort dropped his push pole in the river and simultaneously almost fell out of the canoe. He forgot to drop the anchor, and between the canoe rocking back and forth and Voldemort slipping and sliding, I had little hope of landing my first Atlantic salmon. From all the grunts and groans coming from the back of the canoe, I knew Mark was biting his nails. It was only a matter of time before Mark put Voldemort out of his misery.

Voldemort was doing his best to paddle the canoe as close to the bank as possible so we could get out and fight the salmon from the shore. I was screaming, "Stay in the middle of the damn river!"

I looked up; the covered bridge was only fifty or sixty yards downriver, and my salmon had no intention of slowing down. There was little I could do at the moment. The problem was there was a giant icebreaker pointed upriver, dividing the bridge into two channels, and at this point, I didn't have a clue which side the salmon was going to choose. If it went right, we would be safe, but if the salmon decided it wanted to go left and we were on the right bank, the icebreaker would cut me off. I begged Voldemort to stay in the middle, but he kept digging for the right bank like a stubborn mule. He kept mumbling something about being the guide and knowing what he was doing. Several minutes later, the canoe was safely on the right bank, but the fish's fate was still in question.

The biggest problem I had was the ten-pound tippet. There was only so much pressure I could put on the salmon without breaking him off. To my surprise, the salmon stayed north of the bridge, and now it decided to use the current to its advantage and slug it out. Ten or fifteen minutes later, I was starting to make some progress. The fish was only twenty or twenty-five feet from the bank when out of nowhere, Voldemort charged into the river with a gigantic Atlantic salmon net and tried to net the fish. The next thing I knew, the line was screaming off my reel, the salmon taking back all the line I had spent the last half hour recovering. The same thing happened two or three more times before Mark screamed at him to get the hell out of the water. I kept telling him if he would get behind me and put the damn net down until the fish was ready to net, I would swim the fish into the net. A few minutes later, the salmon slid into the net, but Voldemort seemed angry for some reason. It was as if Mark and I had stolen his thunder. It was a beautiful hen, not a scratch on her, but she was tired, and I was beginning to worry that the fight might have gone on too long. The last thing I wanted to do was accidentally kill a healthy salmon, for any reason, especially for the sake of a few photographs for someone's website. At some point, the insanity has got to stop!

We spent the next ten minutes reviving her, and eventually she swam away with a big push and disappeared into the depths of the Matapédia. I like to believe she survived and managed to lay tens of thousands of eggs over her lifetime. It wasn't a giant salmon, but it was probably in the twenty-two- to maybe twenty-three-pound range. It was a beautiful fish, and considering it was my first Atlantic salmon, all I could do was smile. I was hooked, though honestly, I was hooked the first time I stepped into the Little Cascapédia the previous year. Yes, catching a salmon was important, especially my first one. It's the fundamental reason we spend the time and energy to do this, not to mention the cost. If the Atlantic salmon fisheries of the world have any chance of surviving, we will have to adjust our priorities. One can only hope by the time we have reached this point in life, it should be obvious to everyone.

It Was the Best of Times

FOR SOMEONE WHO LOVES TO CHASE ANADROMOUS FISH, I HAPPEN TO live about as far away from an Atlantic salmon river, or a decent steelhead river, as is possible in the continental United States. I live in Mobile, Alabama. I'm not upset because Alabama is home to some of the best freshwater fishing in the Southeast and could easily be considered the jumping-off point to some of the best saltwater fly fishing south of the Mason-Dixon Line.

I can think of worse things to do in the late afternoon than slowly drifting along the banks of a gorgeous lake, pounding the cattails with micro poppers for giant bluegills and largemouth bass while simultaneously fending off the mosquitoes and listening to the high-pitched caterwauling of red-winged blackbirds.

Still, the lucky among us have at some point found that one, maybe two, species of fish we fell in love with (though my wife uses a repertoire of different words I'm not entirely sure are legitimate synonyms for lucky). For me, those fish are steelhead and Atlantic salmon. For others, it might be tarpon or permit, snook, or redfish. If you held my feet to the proverbial fire, I would have to admit the truth: I also love permit fishing! Essentially that's what this book is about—the three greatest gamefish on the planet, at least from my perspective.

Unfortunately, the pull of the famous steelhead rivers of British Columbia and the Maritime province of Quebec drive me crazy at times. Sometimes I feel like Ulysses lashed to the mast of his ship, struggling to resist the Sirens' songs and the temptation to join them. In my experience, fishermen are attracted to places that are entirely different from where they live or where they grew up. Sometimes, I think it's a combination

A TALE OF THREE FISH

of wanderlust, that itch you can't scratch, and the other side of the fence. Glossy magazine pictures and Saturday morning infomercials lure us in when we're young, and, as with every illicit drug, once we take the bait and experience our first taste, we end up hooked for life.

Forty-six years ago, I caught my first steelhead on the Clackamas River in Oregon. It took two more years before I caught my second one on the Wilson River just east of Tillamook. My first steelhead was relatively small, maybe six or seven pounds dripping wet, but he was a bight fish nonetheless. My second one almost spooled me twice before the guide tailed the fish and slid it back into the river. A large winter steelhead, exponentially bigger than my first, it was in such great shape it might have migrated into the river that very morning. The fish was so full of piss and vinegar that, to be honest, I had little hope of landing it. If it hadn't been for the guide dragging my sorry ass up and down the river, I would have lost the fish.

Little did I know, but I was hooked in a paradox of sorts; I had managed to get myself addicted to a fish that, at the time, was considered almost impossible (or at least extremely difficult) to catch on a fly. Living a few time zones away from the closest steelhead river doesn't improve the odds much either. So naturally it became an obsession. It's been my experience that addiction to anything expensive and elusive can destroy a life if left unchecked. Honestly, I have seen it happen.

Many years later, thanks to the fly-tying genius and imagination of the late Carrie Stevens, I caught my first Atlantic salmon on the Matapédia on a Grey Ghost salmon fly. On the last day, during the last run, on virtually the final cast of a long trip without so much as a tug, I caught a bright salmon in a beautiful location on a once-famous Atlantic salmon river. The dramatic end-of-the-trip timing almost seemed appropriate for such a momentous occasion.

Years earlier, on a ten-day float trip deep in the heart of the Minipi watershed, swinging an original Grey Ghost through a deep tailout, I had managed to hook and land an eight- or nine-pound landlocked salmon. My one regret: The fly, which had been a gift from a close friend, was falling apart by the time we landed the fish. I probably should never have fished that fly, but I think Carrie would have approved. Some flies have a life of their own and, regardless of their value (sentimental or otherwise), need to be fished, just like old bamboo fly rods. Still, when the guide discovered I had destroyed an original Carrie Stevens, he teetered on tears. Or, at least, he pretended to; one never knows with Newfies (an affectionate moniker for Newfoundland guides), as they have a sense of humor all their own. I, on the other hand, was just amazed he even knew who Carrie Stevens was.

In short, I can blame my addiction on my great fortune to have fished some of the most productive steelhead rivers on the West Coast. Of course, having covered a significant fraction of the most productive rivers is not all that impressive anymore, considering that only a handful of great steelhead rivers still survive. Atlantic salmon rivers haven't fared much better. Like most steelhead rivers in California, Oregon, and Washington, the Northeast's Atlantic salmon rivers have all but collapsed. If you're lucky, you can catch a faint whiff of what was but will likely never be again.

The Gaspé Peninsula is the last great stronghold of the Atlantic salmon in North America. Three years ago, Joe Hovious and I had the opportunity to fish Middle Camp on the Grand Cascapédia. Though somewhat less than ideal, the second week of August was the only week available, so we had to content ourselves with the inauspicious dog days of salmon fishing. Believe me, I would have sold my soul to the devil for one or two weeks on the Grand Cascapédia in May, June, or July. Give or take a week here or there, those months are considerably better than August through early October—exponentially more expensive, too. It hasn't always been that way. At one time in the not-so-distant past, if the conditions were right, September produced some of the best Atlantic salmon fishing of the season; the rivers were still thriving with multitudes of Atlantic salmon in the fall. I am sad to say those days are long gone, and without a modern-day miracle, I don't see them returning (but who knows).

What it boils down to is that Atlantic salmon fishing is difficult under the best of situations, but with current population numbers and climate, Atlantic salmon fishing in August is, at best, a crapshoot. Fortunately for us, this particular August happened to be outstanding. We patted ourselves on the back for having paid a fraction of what the trip would have cost the previous three months. And even if we had the money to spare, chances of finding an opening during high season would have been slim to none. Essentially, fly-fishing for Salmo salar remains the sport of kings—except now kings are far and few between and the rod has been passed to the nouveau riche, lending credence to the line from *Midnight in the Garden of Good and Evil* in which Jim Williams informs the writer, John Kelso, "Yes, I am nouveau riche, but then, it's the riche that counts now, isn't it?"

During our auspicious late-summer trip, we constituted a party of six mostly experienced spey fishermen. The river remained relatively high for the season, and the water temperatures still teetered on the chilly side of warm. Over the next six days, we caught thirty-one Atlantic salmon between the six of us. According to the guides, three of them weighed over thirty pounds. Of course, we know the guides would never exaggerate. I won't say they would blatantly lie in hopes of garnering a more substantial tip, but for the sake of argument, they might have been a little short on telling the truth. Then again, the guides could have been nothing more than woodland nymphs that floated in and out of the hardwoods lining the Cascapédia Valley and played harmless tricks on the fishermen. If nothing else, it makes for interesting conversation around the dinner table at night. It gets even more intriguing after dinner when it's time to fill out the logbook. More often than not, the fishermen wait until everyone has either gone to bed or at least had a few drinks. The information you put in the log goes directly to the Cascapedia River Society, essentially the official record-keeper of the Grand Cascapédia for posterity.

Against the odds, this particular trip was one of the most, if not the most, productive Atlantic salmon trips I had ever experienced. One could only wonder what May and June must have been like that year. When it comes to Atlantic salmon, I set the bar relatively low. If I catch one nice fish, I consider the trip a success. If I happen to hook and land two nice fish, I can get a little giddy. And if the gods find it in their heart to bless me with three fish, I might cite a verse or two from Lord Tennyson over dinner. If I happen to have a whisky snifter in my hand, swirling an eighteen-year-old Scotch, I might even start to quote Hemingway. On the other hand, if I get skunked, you might find me curled up in a leather recliner stuffed somewhere in a corner, mumbling something about "my precious" and drinking from the bottle. It's a capricious game we pay to play—and not for the faint of heart!

Case in point, several months later, Joe Hovious, Larry Golightly, Jerry Arni, and I were headed to British Columbia in late October and early November to fish the Bulkley and the Morice River for winter steelhead. The winter runs can be iffy at best. They exist, of course, but unlike Atlantic salmon, in British Columbia, steelhead enter the Skeena drainage in the spring, summer, and fall. In late October and early November, the winter fish start to show up. The dates the fish arrive fluctuate from year to year, depending on dozens of variables. Depending on the year, October and November can be relatively mild; then again, it can be brutally cold. It's like everything else that has to do with anadromous fish; it's a crapshoot at best. Mother Nature can be a fickle lady; she plays by her set of rules, not yours, and from what I have seen, she could care less if you catch a fish or not.

So when you finally get the chance to fish one of the premier steelhead drainages on the planet, and you ask, "How's the fishing," the response you're looking for is, "It's the best fishing we have experienced in the last fifty years." The last thing you want to hear is, "It's the worst fishing we have experienced in the last fifty years."

The "best fishing in fifty years" often occurs when the salmon run is almost nonexistent and the fisheries biologist decides to shut down the commercial fishing fleet at the mouth of the Skeena. When that happens, the steelhead runs can be phenomenal, assuming it's a good year for steelhead. Not all runs are created equal, and the numbers of steelhead that migrate up the Skeena vary from year to year. Shutting down the commercial fleets means that, for all practical purposes, you shouldn't have any bycatch; still, it doesn't necessarily guarantee a good steelhead season. Then again, I have no idea how much poaching goes on throughout the drainage. I haven't seen any, but that doesn't mean it doesn't exist.

The "worst fishing in fifty years" seems to happen when the salmon are plentiful enough to open the commercial fishing season. When that happens, the number of steelhead in the Skeena drainage plummets.

Coincidence? Maybe, but I doubt it. Until the British Columbia government decides to track and count the bycatch, we will never have anything but anecdotal evidence. Similarly, the number of fish taken by the Indigenous tribes each year should be counted. Several wildlife biologists have told me that they do their best to release the steelhead, and at some level the Indigenous tribes understand that a live steelhead is good for business. I have had the pleasure of eating a freshly caught steelhead and can appreciate the temptation. Like a fresh King Salmon, a steelhead is delicious, but eating a fresh steelhead these days might be considered sacrilegious.

Once I am committed to a trip, I try my best to ignore the data leading up to it. For one reason, I probably booked the trip the previous year, and just because the fishing is slow doesn't necessarily mean the lodge owner or local guide is going to refund my hard-earned dollars. Also, the Skeena drainage is vast, and even at the best of times the fishing is difficult, so whether it's teeming with fish or the fish are far and few between, the experience promises to be similar either way. Over the years, I've tried to convince myself that the fish are secondary, and that it's the experience that counts. Of course, we all know that's a juicy rationalization we employ to help us sleep better at night when we haven't touched a fish in days.

The Skeena drainage is a living, breathing ecosystem. To make things a little more challenging, it's enormous. It would take more than one lifetime to learn the entire system's ins and outs or even just its more famous tributaries. The river system is continuously changing. Learning the ins and outs of each river is almost impossible if you don't live there. Not only does the river change every year, but it also changes drastically throughout the year. The water levels sometimes fluctuate daily, and, depending on the rain or lack thereof, the river can rise or fall during the same day.

If you booked a trip the previous year, hitting the timing just right becomes a long shot at best. Hell, even if you booked it the same year, it remains a matter of chance. You do what most die-hard steelhead fishermen do: You roll the dice and take what the river gives you. Like Santa Claus, the river knows if you have been naughty or nice.

Only a few months earlier, Joe and I had returned from one of the best Atlantic salmon fishing trips any fisherman could ask for. Chances of duplicating the same experience three months later, 2,600 miles away on the Pacific coast of Canada, seemed a little too much to expect. We were staying at the Far West Frontier Steelhead Lodge. It's a beautiful lodge located on the banks of the Bulkley River: a prime location and jumping-off point for multiple fisheries. The lodge has an excellent reputation; the hospitality is off the charts, and the guides are knowledgeable and seem to love what they are doing. It's been our experience that everyone at the lodge works incredibly hard to make sure their customers enjoy themselves, and that's about all you can ask for these days—except maybe one or two more Tim Hortons. (One can never have too many.)

That being said, rumors had been floating around the small town of Smithers all summer about the incredible number of fish in the system. The only problem was the water was lower than anyone had ever seen it in years. The fishing was going to be tough; at least that was the prevailing attitude around camp when we arrived.

After everyone had unpacked and wolfed down lunch, we still had half a day of free fishing to look forward to. The trip consisted of seven nights and six days fishing. The fishing officially started the next day, so the next four or five hours were technically a freebie. It didn't take our group long to change into our waders and jump into trucks to hit the road or climb into jet boats to blast off up or down the Bulkley. For our part, Joe and I leisurely moseyed down the path to the stretch of river behind the lodge. I have to admit I felt a little cheated, but what the hell, it's hard to complain about a free day of fishing. I remember walking down to the river and just staring into what was left of the Bulkley. What typically looked like a mighty river had been reduced to a quaint mountain stream I could have essentially walked across without getting my thighs wet.

Joe started low, and I went high. The guide went with me for some reason. I don't mind fishing alone. I much prefer it. Maybe he thought I was going to freeze to death. It did not take me long to realize that I was a tad underdressed for the occasion. I had one pair of lightweight thermal underwear, a lightweight polypuff jacket, and a benny. I hadn't even brought a pair of gloves. I kept telling myself if it got too cold, I would just walk back to my cabin and put on some more clothes.

On my third cast I hooked and landed a rather nice steelhead. Some people might have called it a ripe tomato, but a fish is a fish, and they are all beautiful. Several casts later, I hooked another fish, this time with shoulders. After ten or fifteen minutes, I landed my second steelhead—and I hadn't been in the river forty-five minutes. Following this auspicious start, we walked back down the river to where Joe was fishing to see how he was faring.

The guide and I spent so much time talking about the number of fish in the system that we didn't notice Joe was into what looked like a nice fish. He was stumbling down the river doing his best to stay vertical. It's incredible how fast a big fish can spool you, and the worst part about it is there is absolutely nothing you can do except go with the flow and hope you don't fall on your face. Not only is that cold, but it's also embarrassing. By the time we managed to catch up with Joe, the fish was starting to tire, and there was little left to do but tail the fish and release it. It was a fresh fish. I have no real idea how long it had been in the system, but it was a bright fish with a hint of rose down its flanks. The cheeks were starting to color, and when the guide finally released the steelhead, it bolted downriver as if nothing had happened.

I was really getting cold at this point, and I asked the guide if we could start a fire somewhere along the bank. Once the guide returned from the lodge with a truck full of firewood, Joe kept fishing, and I spent the rest of the evening sitting by the fire. I was freezing, although I didn't want the guide to know I was stupid enough to travel to the Pacific Rim dressed only for a Scottish summer. Something told me, though, he had already figured it out.

Nights come early in British Columbia this late in the year. By the end of the first day, a toasty cabin, a potent cocktail, and a hot shower sounded wonderful. I had no idea what to expect the next day. In situations like this, there is little you can do except take it day by day. The following morning I heard a knock at the door and was met by one of the friendly staff with a hot coffee. I could get used to this. To my surprise, it looked as though it had been snowing all night. Several inches of fresh snow covered the ground. Luckily, not enough snow had fallen to blow out the river, but enough to raise it an inch or two. Since we knew (and had perfunctorily confirmed for ourselves the previous day) that the river held a tremendous number of fish but could use some fresh water, we looked upon the white dusting as a good omen, mine tampered with a bit of frostbite.

It continued to drizzle or snow every night. That's Canadian manners for you. Only occasionally was the weather so uncouth as to continue snowing throughout the day. The river continued to rise several inches every day; the fishing was off the charts, and it didn't really matter where we fished. Some of the fishermen fished the Bulkley, others the Canyon; some floated the upper Skeena. A few of us rolled out of bed in the middle of the night once, loaded one of the trucks, hooked up one of the jet boats, and headed up to the Dean. Everyone was catching fish. It had become the norm, not the exception. The water ran clear, the guides were dialed in, and the rivers were loaded with fish. It was the first time I remember waking up in the morning knowing that I was going to get into a few steelhead, possibly lots of steelhead. It was as close as any fisherman can come to nirvana with their feet still firmly planted on terra firma.

The first morning Joe and I fished the upper Morice. To be honest, I asked for it. I love the Morice. It's a beautiful river and, late in the season, depending on the water level, the fishing can be fantastic. I fished up top with Joe fifty or sixty yards below me when I hooked what I thought was a tree limb. The current ran fast, and there were fallen trees everywhere. Though I pulled with everything I had, I couldn't move what I had hooked but a few inches at a time. When I backed off on the pressure, the limb went right back to where it started from. After a few minutes of back-and-forth, I was actually trying to break the fly off. The guide finally came up and wanted to know what was going on. When I tried to explain, he just laughed and asked, "How do you know you don't have a fish on?"

I scoffed and said something to the effect that if this was a fish, it had to be a monster. Still, I abandoned the idea of breaking my line and continued the back-and-forth for the next ten minutes or so. Finally, my tree limb started moving down the river, slowly. Then it occurred to me that I might have hooked a big fish in the tail or the dorsal fin. I kept thinking if I had snagged the fish in one of the pectoral fins, I probably could have turned it, or at the very least aggravated it a little. The water was rather deep along the far bank, and the fish never came up. About that time, Joe started laughing and said, "There is no way you have the fish hooked in the mouth; he has to be snagged."

It was hard to argue with him. For all practical purposes, I still thought I might have a tree limb in tow. Then the fish decided it had had enough of the back-and-forth and bolted downstream. Twenty minutes later, the guide tailed my fish. Of course, the steelhead was hooked in the mouth. I had no idea what everyone was worried about. I graced Joe with a superior smile, as though I had known all along. My expression might have taken on a hint of a triumphant sneer when the guide looked back and announced, "This is the first legitimate eighteen- to twenty-pound steelhead I've seen this year."

A few minutes later, we started a fire to sit around, warm up with hot coffee, and shoot the breeze. Joe kept mumbling something about me taking his fish and explaining in great detail how my steelhead had clearly been headed his way. To hear Joe tell it, you'd believe he'd already made meaningful eye contact and set up a date with the fish before I so rudely butted in. In short, Joe only lasted half an hour sitting around the fire; he stood up, grabbed his rod, and made his way back downstream. Even as he walked away he kept lecturing me about stealing his fish. I don't think he had made but three casts before he hooked into a nice fish. I stayed near the fire and enjoyed watching Joe fight the fish; he really is an excellent spey fisherman. I have several friends that I consider world-class spey casters—people like Chris Anderson, Mark Lance, Jeff Bright, Greg Mau, among others—but Joe has one of the sweetest casts I have ever seen. When Joe is in the zone, his casting borders on artistic. Of course, he would never admit it.

I've tried throughout the years to duplicate his stroke with little or no success. Of course, Joe lives in the Northeast, where he gets to practice his craft on any number of great rivers. As I mentioned above, I live in Mobile, and for all practical purposes, I could be the only spey fisherman in the great state of Alabama. On a good year, I might get to spend six or seven weeks chasing steelhead and Atlantic salmon. Other than that, I spend the year with a single-handed fly rod in tow, mostly sight-fishing for snook and tarpon and the occasional bonefish. At least a few times a year, you will find me staked out on a flat somewhere in Central America or the Florida Keys chasing permit.

Trying to transition from a single-handed fly rod to a spey rod and a running river can be difficult. The transition from Atlantic salmon fishing to spey fishing the Pacific Northwest for steelhead is challenging on so many levels. Atlantic salmon fishing traditionally requires floating lines, wispy leaders, and tiny flies. On the other hand, winter steelhead fishing typically requires bulky running lines, ten feet or more of T-20, a stout leader, and a weighted fly with an uncanny resemblance to a saltwater jig. I don't think it's necessarily the constant cold that keeps the faint of heart away; it's the heavy gear that's required to dredge up a winter steelhead. On some level, you almost have to be a little touched to enjoy winter steelhead fishing. I love it! I have no idea what that says about my fellow compañeros and me.

The days seemed to fly by, the fishing was outstanding, and everyone was catching fish. I'm not going to describe the number and size of fish we caught that week. I doubt you would believe me anyway, but it was epic, by far the best week of steelhead fishing I have ever experienced. And judging by the enthusiasm around the lodge that week, everyone seemed to be having the time of their life.

I think most of the guests understood on some level that they might never experience a week like this again. Unfortunately, fishing is fishing, and it's never the same from year to year. In a way, that's the point in all of this. If we slew fish every time we went fishing, we'd probably give it up and move on to something less expensive.

It was snowing hard when we left the lodge that last morning, so we knew it would probably be snowing harder up top. It was going to be a cold, wet day. Of course, with all the high-tech clothing stuffed in our waterproof travel bags and half a cord of firewood, one might assume we were headed for the far Arctic, either that or some half-ass astronauts on our way to colonize Mars. Looking back, we might have been a little overprepared. Fortunately, we were in a rather large jet boat, and even though we had bags scattered everywhere, there was still plenty of room to move around. We didn't have to run a long way that day. It was the last day of the season, and the guides had to somehow trailer the boats at the end of the day in deep snow and drag them back to the lodge.

A half hour later, the guide shut the engine down, slid the jet boat up on a gravel bar, and then threw the anchor onto the sandy beach. This was the first time I had ever fished this section of the river. It was beautiful in so many ways (I say that every time I fish the Morice, and it's beginning to sound like a broken record, which I know reads like an overused cliché, but it sounds exponentially better than saying a broken digital download). The truth is, the Morice is the kind of river a steelhead fisherman dreams about, especially late in the year. It's the quintessential steelhead river. At some point in life, every die-hard steelhead fisherman should have the opportunity to fish the Morice in the fall. As with the pilgrimage to Mecca, it should be mandatory to visit the Morice in prime time at least once in your lifetime.

We anchored the jet boat at the bottom of a long run, just above a blistering tailout that took a hard ninety-degree left turn at the bottom. The river took another hard right at the top around a massive logjam that had to be at least a hundred feet tall. It reminded me of the great wall of Troy—that is, assuming there was a great wall of Troy. (If I remember correctly, Homer also gave us the story of Atlantis. I can only assume that Hollywood gave us Aquaman.) If you hooked a big fish that decided to head upriver, there was little you could do. There was absolutely no way of getting around the logjam without a boat or a helicopter, and even though we had a perfectly good boat anchored downstream, you're not allowed to fish out of it on the Morice.

There was a lot of water to cover, and then the obligatory campfire, lunch, and after-lunch bullshit session that could go on for hours. Of course, that depended on the number of fish you hooked or caught that morning. I could see us spending the entire day here. The last day of a fishing trip tends to take on a life of its own. If the week had gone as planned and you managed to catch a few fish, the last day is tradition-ally a time to shut it down and put the week in perspective. Sometimes fishermen become obsessed with catching another fish; they forget to slow down and appreciate the small things in life. On the other hand, if the fishing was on the poor side that week, then the last day can be somewhat stressful.

I always let Joe decide where he wants to start, the top or the bottom of the run. Personally, I couldn't care less. Joe was quiet for a moment; he was waiting to see if he could figure out where I wanted to start before making his decision. Finally, after weighing all the variables, Joe decided to start at the bottom, and why not? It looked fishy, and I had no real idea what the water looked like up top, not to mention it was almost a quarter mile to the top of the run. The landscape was breathtaking. The trees were covered with ice and snow, and the river seemed to be rising. A mature golden eagle and several immature birds we circling overhead in search of breakfast. As I made my way to the top, I kept thinking, what a great place to camp and spend the week fishing. Then it dawned on me: I was walking down the beach by myself in the middle of "Grizzly Central."

At any moment, a six- or seven-hundred-pound grizzly could quickly come crashing down out of the woods and chew my ass off. You laugh, but it's happened to other fishermen. It's something no one wants to talk about. Reality starts to set in at some point, though, and finally you realize there's very little you can do about it anyway, so you go fishing and do your best not to think about it. I would be just another name on a long list of poor souls who were mauled in the Morice drainage. It happened to Gary Limage. Fortunately, Gary survived, even though he was severely mauled and left for dead before one of the locals discovered him in a drainage ditch along the side of the road. Gary was one of the most experienced bush pilots on the planet. He spent his life camping and fishing throughout Alaska, most of it deep in grizzly country. No one knows exactly why it happened, or if his experience with bears saved his life. I can only assume it had to help.

The guide was several hundred yards downriver, and the fact that he had a gun and several cans of bear repellent in the boat didn't do me any good. To make things worse, I was about to walk into the river with my back to the woods, oblivious to the world on land. Of course, I never saw a grizzly bear that day, never heard one, but it didn't stop my imagination from going into overdrive. It's a little sobering when you finally come to terms with the fact that you are no longer the top predator in the ecosystem. In fact, as local species go, you are relatively low on the totem pole.

Other than the occasional adrenaline spike here and there, it was incredibly peaceful. I made a few short casts along the bank in case there were any fish holding in the shallow water. I made swing after swing until I finally reached the logjam on the other shore. It's funny how your cast always seems better on the last day of a trip. I was dialed in and wasn't thinking about my cast or anything else really. I was doing my best to absorb the river and the surrounding forest. It's a sensory overload at times, and almost spiritual on some level. I made one more cast toward the logjam and then threw in a few mends upriver to slow the swing down and get the fly as close to the bottom as possible. Suddenly, about ten or fifteen feet downriver, I felt the tug, but this was no everyday tug. It almost took the spey rod out of my hands. It felt like a large fish, and I was about to holler to Joe to net my fish as he went by. Then I heard Joe yell, "Have you got a fish on?"

Then for some reason or other I yelled back, "No, I am stuck on a rock—of course I have a fish on."

Joe started laughing and said something to the guide, and the guide threw the net back into the boat and started my way as if he was kicking a tin can down the street without a care in the world. I had very little backing left on the reel when the guide finally realized I had a big fish on and not a rock. I was running down the river, tripping and falling on the small boulders, when the line fell slack. The fly had pulled. It was as if someone reached in and cut my heart out with a spoon. It took what seemed like hours reeling all the slack line back in. The guide walked up and said something to the effect: "That was a hot fish. I would have been here faster, but Joe said you were stuck on a rock."

It was hard to complain. At this point, Joe and I had already had a great week, and according to the "Bear," this was nothing more than "the lemon next to the pie."

In reality, it was a hot fish, but just how big is hard to determine. The Morice is a fast river, and it's been my experience that steelhead, like all gamefish, instinctively know how to use the current to their advantage.

For a fish with a brain the size of a pea, they seem awful intelligent to me. I finally retrieved all my fly line and headed back to where I had begun with the guide in tow. I made several more casts and hooked another fish in the same spot. Fifteen minutes later, the guide tailed the fish; we took a few pics, released the bright steelhead, and watched it swim away. Several minutes later, I hooked another fish in the same spot; there was no telling how many fish were stacked up next to the logjam. I landed the second fish virtually in the same manner as I did the previous fish. Ten or fifteen minutes later, I hooked a screaming locomotive, but this one went upstream, and no matter how much pressure I put on the fish, I couldn't slow it down. I was deep into my backing, and it still wouldn't slow down. All the guide could say was, "Damn, that's a huge fish."

By this time, I had begun to use a few tarpon tricks—to no avail. I gave the fish some down and dirty to the right and then some down and dirty to the left in hopes of making him change direction or at least jump a few times to expend some energy. The truth is the fish was too far upriver for that tactic to have any meaningful effect on it. Then I begged the guide to go down and get the boat and run me around the logjam. He kept mumbling something about not being able to fish out of a boat on the Morice and if he got caught, he would lose his guide's license, or something to that effect. Then, just like with the first steelhead, my fly line fell slack. Then the guide said something about switching places with my buddy and letting him in on the action. I said, "You're kidding, right? I don't know that guy. I just met him a few days ago."

Then I informed him, "You do know this is a gift from the gods, and if I walk away, I may never catch another steelhead, and it will be all your fault."

In the end, I went down and told Joe to switch places. I even told him what fly to use and where to fish. I made several casts where Joe had initially been fishing, but my mojo was gone. I cut my fly off and reeled in my line. It was probably better I didn't hook another steelhead in Joe's spot; he never would have let me live it down. To make a long story short, Joe fished in the same place I did with the same fly for over an hour and never got so much as a tug. There is a lesson to be learned here: Never, ever upset the gods. Take what they give you and be grateful, if not humble.

The lodge was rocking that night; everyone had a wonderful trip, give or take one or two people who, for some reason or other, couldn't seem to let their hair hang down. If you couldn't get excited after the previous week of fishing, then there is little hope for you. Then again, it could have been caused by nothing more than the lack of quality bourbon.

Is it any wonder, then, that I am addicted to fly-fishing for steelhead and Atlantic salmon, even though I have to travel far, crossing over lots of water full of different types of fish, to get to them? It's the occasional win that keeps a gambler hooked. A win has the same effect on fishermen. It's the smell of the campfire, the bantering camaraderie; it's seeing wild places and being reminded that although we have certainly hurt the planet, it's not too late to save and restore what we have left. It's too precious to squander!

It Was the Worst of Times

When I look back, give or take a few bumps here and there, 2018 was a great year to be on the water. The economy was on fire, the stock market was skyrocketing, and the future looked promising. Travel was easy, the fishing was off the charts, and everyone seemed to be in great spirits—and why not? It was hands down the best steelhead and Atlantic salmon season I can remember.

Then again, maybe it was too good. We had every reason to expect 2019 to be the same. Assuming that you considered the previous year the pinnacle of success, the problem was there was nowhere to go but down. Unfortunately, we had made the mistake of forgetting the days and sometimes weeks that didn't go as planned. Fishermen are gullible if not delusional at times. If things go right, we have a habit of looking at the world through a pair of rose-colored glasses. Then we pat ourselves on the back and take the credit for the excellent fishing. We forget the contribution of the outfitter and the local guide in all of this, much less the fish. Then again, it could never have happened in the first place if you hadn't got off the couch and gone fishing. That in itself is reason enough to enjoy the occasional pat on the back. In retrospect, last year should have been an omen of things to come.

Unfortunately, 2019 turned out to be the opposite of the previous year. There would be a string of hurricanes that decimated a significant portion of the Caribbean and the Bahamas, laying waste to some of the best bonefish lodges in the tropics—not to mention hundreds if not thousands of private homes and small businesses.

Later that year, multiple hurricanes pounded the Gulf Coast from Texas to the Florida Panhandle, sweeping away some of the most abundant aquatic vegetation along the Gulf Coast. Don't get me wrong; traditionally, hurricanes are good for the environment. I know that's hard to swallow, especially if it happened to be your property. On the other hand, most Americans want to live either on the water or as close to the water as they can afford. If you live along the Gulf Coast, it's never a case of *if*. It's a case of *when* the next Category 5 hurricane comes screaming off the coast of Africa like a runaway locomotive.

Hurricanes and tropical storms have battered coastlines throughout the tropics for the last ten thousand years, depending on whom you ask. Powerful hurricanes have been sculpting and reworking the coastal environments that provide the landscapes fishermen find appealing long before the first condominium was conceived. Of course, tectonic drift and the occasional asteroid might have done a lot of the heavy lifting. The entire process is humbling when you consider humans have so little control of the climate. It starts with the earth's tilt, the planet's wobble, and the shape of the earth's orbit around the sun. Unless you happen to be a Greek Titan named Atlas, there is very little you can do except sit back and take what comes next.

The powerful winds and strong tides created by hurricanes and tropical storms flush out the estuaries and disperse the detritus that deprive the water of oxygen. If not, it would continue to decompose, and all the grass would die, taking with it the majority of the biodiversity that once thrived there. Once the grass is gone, the bait dies off or moves on, forcing the local gamefish to find another neighborhood in which to make a living.

It's essential to understand the difference between the hand of man and Mother Nature. Leave her alone, and she thrives. Interfere with Mother Nature, and she traditionally bites back. It doesn't take a genius to notice that most of the environmental damage along the Gulf Coast has been done by humans over the last several hundred years, not hurricanes. You don't have to look any farther than the Mississippi River.

In his infinite wisdom, man destroyed the majority of the wetlands and estuaries along the Mississippi. He then used the plow to convert the land along the river and its tributaries to farmland. Today the Mississippi River is nothing more than a drainage ditch from the Canadian border and beyond to the Mississippi River Delta. The amount of pollution that gets flushed down the big river every year is staggering. It has created a dead zone in the Gulf of Mexico that covers six or seven thousand square miles beginning at the mouth of the Mississippi River and extending west to the upper Texas coast, depending on the season. It's essentially the size of the state of New Jersey. The dead zone is caused by nutrient enrichment from the Mississippi, particularly nitrogen and phosphorous used in agriculture. The laws of unintended consequences strike again. Then again, the idea that no one understood the consequences beforehand is a little far-fetched.

As much as 60 percent of the aquatic vegetation along the coast has been destroyed over the last thirty years, with no end in sight. The Louisiana Delta is losing as much as twenty meters of aquatic vegetation per year. The "Big Muddy" has been running on average at seventeen feet above sea level and sometimes higher for several years. It's no wonder the city of New Orleans starts to hyperventilate at the mere mention of a tropical storm. The levees are useless when the water level gets above twenty-one feet. It's a little disconcerting considering New Orleans at the best of times lies two to eight feet below sea level, and yet by some miracle, NOLA survives, and hordes of drunken tourists still rock the night away on Bourbon Street.

The Mississippi and the Louisiana Delta are known for their world-class red fishing; the area is also home to millions of ducks and shorebirds. The red fishing has held up so far, but how long that will last is anyone's guess. Between the dead zones, loss of habitat, and the drilling and refineries along the Gulf Coast, one has little hope for the future. It's an environmental disaster waiting to happen; then again, one might wonder, how much worse could it get? Believe me when I tell you it could get much worse.

South Florida has become ground zero for one of the most highly debated environmental disasters of the twenty-first century. Considering the number of people and animals that have been exposed to the toxic runoff from Lake Okeechobee, it could be the worst environmental disaster since the Three Mile Island reactor meltdown. The atrocity was the damming, diking, and then draining of the Everglades in the first place; the tragedy is simply the consequences of the atrocity and the people that let it happen.

It's as if the agriculture and cattle industry have teamed up and conspired with the state and federal government to destroy what's left of South Florida's once world-class fishing. Since the late 1800s man has done his best to drain the Florida Everglades for agriculture and urban development, and some biologists suggest that only 2 percent of the original ecosystem is truly intact. The problem has always been corrupt state and local government and the South Florida Water Management District (SFWD) aided by the US Army Corps of Engineers. For six thousand years, water flowed south down the Kissimmee floodplain and into Lake Okeechobee, which supplied the Everglades with clean water. The water is used to replenish the Floridian aquifer, one of the largest freshwater aquifers on the planet, and the much smaller Biscayne aquifer. Unfortunately, the lack of fresh water has already caused massive issues with saltwater intrusion. It's become a serious problem considering that three million Dade County residents get their drinking water directly from the Biscayne aquifer.

Mother Nature always comes back to bite you on the ass! It's the one constant in the universe. To create enough dry land for the explosion of people migrating to South Florida, the state had to drain as much as 80 percent of the Everglades, roughly seven-million-plus acres of fertile wetlands along the East Coast and central Florida. And that was only the beginning.

Unfortunately, it became the norm, and to some extent is still prevalent today. The agriculture industry uses roughly two-million-plus acres of what was once one of the most fertile ecosystems on the planet. The cattle industry uses four and a half million acres of pristine habitat, give or take a few acres.

In 1960 C. Farris Bryant, a newly elected Democratic governor, gave the thumbs-up to channel the Kissimmee River. He was also a strong proponent of the once doomed to fail "Cross Florida Barge Canal." To drain the excess water, the Army Corps of Engineers first had to channel the Kissimmee River and remove the oxbows, again eliminating precious water that was needed to refill the Biscayne and Floridian aquifers. Years later, after the oxbows had been removed or filled in, the public screamed bloody murder. Eventually, the state government had to devise a plan for fear of losing their jobs: to restore the Kissimmee Basin to its original grandeur. It's far from complete, but to be honest, it's better than it was, though nowhere what it was before the politicians and robber barons aided by greedy developers sweeping in from the Northeast trashed it in first place. Of course, it took exponentially more state and federal money to undo the damage that had already been done by the Corps. It's ironic: The Corps took federal tax dollars to destroy the Kissimmee River and then it took more federal tax dollars to restore the damage. And yet no one was ever charged for the crimes against nature.

Like the Mississippi River, the Kissimmee Basin's yearly flooding is what created the incredibly fertile land in the first place. To have enough water in reserve for the agriculture industry, the Corps dammed and diked Lake Okeechobee's lower stretches. By the time the Corps had finished the dirty deed, as little as 30 percent of the water was allowed to flow south. For all practical purposes, the Everglades were left to die. What you see today is just a fraction of the original watershed. An ecosystem that once enveloped over eight million acres of fertile wetlands has been reduced to a few layers of mud and limestone and a few puddles of water here and there.

Some biologists estimate that the Everglades has lost as much as 70 percent of its biomass, including 90 percent of its once famous birdlife. Atrocities like draining, damming, diking, and indirect (or in some cases direct) pollution has been going on for so long in South Florida that it's considered SOP (standard operating procedure) by the South Florida Water Management District and the politicians in Tallahassee. At every opportunity, they continue to give lip service to the Everglades Reclamation Project to get reelected. Few of the politicians in Tallahassee were born or even raised in the state of Florida. I doubt any of them could articulate the problems facing the Kissimmee River Basin, Lake Okeechobee, and the Florida Everglades, or the Ten Thousand Islands, much less fix the damage. Even more unsettling, the money set aside by the federal government for many of these reclamation projects seems to have disappeared from the state coffers. There appears to be little if any accountability these days. Have you ever noticed that politicians never get prosecuted regardless of the severity of the crimes against the environment? Hell, they rarely get prosecuted for anything, much less for the trail of environmental atrocities they leave behind when they eventually leave office.

Like the Mississippi River, Lake Okeechobee is dying a slow death from the same types of pollution that are killing the Louisiana Delta. Pesticides, fertilizers, insecticides, herbicides and excess nitrogen, and tremendous amounts of phosphate used by the citrus and sugarcane industries is devastating what's left of the great lake. In the summer, the temperature rises and creates tremendous algal blooms, until Okeechobee is ready to burst at its seams. The South Florida Water Management District then releases the polluted water into the Saint Lucie River on Florida's east coast and the Caloosahatchee River on the west coast. The dumping has been going on for years; unfortunately, it's getting exponentially worse every year, with no end in sight.

In the summer of 2018, it was as if someone fired a small ICBM into Charlotte Harbor. The SFWD opened the locks on both coasts. The polluted water from Lake Okeechobee flowed with impunity. The Caloosahatchee turned brown and then dumped millions of gallons of contaminated water into Charlotte Harbor, which eventually flowed into the open Gulf. It went on for months; it was the perfect storm. Southwest Florida was already experiencing one of the worst red tides in recorded history, which, combined with the prolific algal blooms, destroyed the majority of Charlotte Harbor's biomass and the beaches as far north as Sarasota and as far south as Naples. The combination of the toxic spill and the existing red tide killed umpteen millions of pounds of fish, whales, sea turtles, manatees, and, for the first time in recent history, it devastated many species of wading birds in record numbers.

Months after the spill began to dissipate and the red tide died off, I took six fishermen down to Sanibel to chase snook on the beach. We walked the beaches day after day, sometimes eight to ten hours a day, and never saw a snook, much less caught one. I spent hours walking the back side of Sanibel Island, trying to find a few remaining grass flats in hopes of catching a few sea trout. The seagrasses were gone—I mean entirely wiped out. For the most part, it was a sterile environment. The terrible stench hung around until late April into early May 2019.

Of course, we all want to blame the politicians, and they deserve a significant portion of the blame, but in reality, it's our fault, too. It should never have happened in the first place. It happened because we let it happen. We sat by and allowed the carpetbaggers and developers to trash one of the most unique ecosystems on the planet, and they're still doing it.

Mother Nature is resilient, if nothing else. Little by little, the beaches started to clear, the bait began to show, and by the end of the year, things were looking up. It was far from perfect, but nonetheless it was an improvement. Unfortunately, it will take decades to rehabilitate the once fertile estuaries that at one time lined the southwest coast of Florida—if that's even possible. We may have crossed the point of no return, and what you see now is the norm, not the exception. It certainly hasn't slowed down development or population growth, especially on Florida's west coast.

There is only one real answer: buy out the agriculture and cattle industry, then remove the dams and dikes on Okeechobee and let the water flow south to restore as much as the Everglades and Florida Bay as possible. It sounds simplistic, and I understand it will never happen. Even today, December 15, 2020, the State of Florida is still dumping massive amounts of polluted water into the Saint Lucie River and the Caloosahatchee River with no real plan, much less any commitment, to solving the problems. If something's not done soon, we may lose it all.

Summer was almost over, and I hadn't even touched a fish so far. I was looking forward to getting back to Middle Camp on the Grand Cascapédia and hopefully repeating last year's Atlantic salmon trip. There was little left to do but to forget the miserable spring and early summer and move on. Unfortunately, some things get indelibly burned into your memory.

Atlantic salmon fishing these days is anything but consistent. It's mainly because of all the environmental issues that affect the maritime province of Quebec, not to mention the millions of striped bass that the provincial government and the Forest Ministry released into the Saint Lawrence Seaway. As if the Atlantic salmon doesn't have enough problems already. Under the right circumstances, you can hook and land a thirty-pound Atlantic salmon then move downriver ten feet and hook and land a twenty-pound striped bass in the same pool. I know you think that's an exaggeration of sorts (and maybe so), but it's not far from the truth.

At some point someone needs to stop the merry-go-round and ask how long the insanity will last. The adult salmon are not necessarily in danger, but what happens when the smolt finally decide to return to the open ocean? The striped bass will devour the majority of the smolt. Considering we are only playing with a fraction of the number of Atlantic salmon that once migrated up the Grand Cascapédia, the striped bass represents a clear and present danger to the future of Atlantic salmon fishing on the Gaspé. Yet it's almost impossible to get anyone to talk about it. Who knows, like South Florida, maybe we are long past the point of no return. Like all environmental nightmares, denial is the first sign you have a real problem. Ignoring the problem only exacerbates the situation. By the time the politicians who created the problem in the first place are held accountable for their atrocities, they have moved on or, even worse, been promoted.

A few weeks later, I picked up Joe Hovious in Connecticut just outside Sandy Hook, and we started our annual migration north. Little did I know at the time, but this would be our last trip to the Grand Cascapédia, at least for the near future.

Middle Camp is an old-world salmon lodge tucked along the banks of the Grand Cascapédia. It's a beautiful lodge with an incredible reputation for big fish. It's the kind of fishing lodge you could spend a week at even if you didn't fish. The food is outstanding, and the service is second to none. As for the guides, all I can say is, guides are guides, and Canadian guides are unique if nothing else. From my perspective, the guides at Middle Camp know the river and the salmon's habits as well or better than any guides I have fished with on the Gaspé. I know that sounds like a juicy rationalization, and to honest, it is. That said, Middle Camp is the crème de la crème of Atlantic salmon lodges, and the Grand Cascapédia is considered one of the finest (if not the finest) Atlantic salmon rivers in North America.

Our first day on the river set the tone for the days to come. The river was low, the water temperature climbed daily, and the fish sulked. We fished four straight days without so much as a tug. Fortunately, I eventually caught one Atlantic salmon. I had been sitting on a series of long flat rocks that jutted out into the river and dropped off to what seemed like a bottomless pool. The pool was crystal clear, and salmon were stacked up at the head of the pool, just enjoying life as if they didn't have a care in the world. Joe had been swinging fly after fly over them for what seemed like hours. He must have changed flies dozens of times and never moved a fish. I was having a cup of coffee and shooting the bull with the guides. Joe kept looking over his left shoulder, trying to talk me into taking over, but I had no desire to stand on the same rock Joe was standing on and fish over the same fish for the next several hours. After all, there is something to be said about slowing down and enjoying the moment. You know, be one with the rock. I was enjoying the company of the guides and the warm sun. I was so comfortable I was ready to take a nap.

Joe finally gave up and climbed onto the rocks, collapsing beside me. We discussed the possibilities of going back to camp for a long nap and hitting it hard later that evening when the sun eased down over the rim of the valley. The guides wouldn't have anything to do with that idea. They finally coaxed Joe into moving down the pool and giving the tailout a try. I put the spey rod down and picked up a single-handed fly rod with a rather elaborate bomber the size of a small squirrel dressed in a multitude of colors that one might find in a box of Crayola crayons. I walked down and proceeded to strip out twenty or thirty feet of line when the guide started barking out orders, something about starting short.

Then Joe's guide casually mentioned something about the big salmon lying at my feet. I had about two feet of fly line out the tip of the fly rod. There wasn't a chance in hell that this big buck was going to rise to one of the ugliest flies I have ever seen, much less take it with me standing only a few feet away. I dropped the bomber three or four feet up current and let it float drag-free downstream directly over the salmon's head. The salmon started to rise. I still didn't give it much chance. Then the fish gently rolled, crushed my fly, and headed downstream. I had fly line lying everywhere. The guides started laughing so hard that one of them slipped on a wet rock and almost fell in the water. It served him right; I was in complete control of the situation.

Then in the background, I could hear Joe screaming something about me poaching his fish. To make things worse, it *was* Joe's guide that had spotted the fish and told me to cast to it. There wasn't much I could say at the moment. For some reason, Joe is always accusing me of poaching his fish. I can never really tell if he is serious or just kidding. The whole scenario seemed somewhat confusing. The two guides were simultaneously criticizing my technique, or maybe they were praising my approach? It's tough to tell with Canadian guides sometimes. Ten or fifteen minutes later, the guide tailed the fish, held it up high for the world to see, and then released the rather large buck into the river. I could have pulled out my camera bag and made a big deal about it, but sometimes discretion is the better part of valor. I grabbed my fly rod and climbed back up on the rocks, poured myself another cup of coffee, and tried to take a short nap.

I have no real idea why the Atlantic salmon took my fly and ignored Joe's fly all morning. I could come up with a half dozen tired old platitudes that are nothing more than random clichés used thousands of times to make people feel better. I could wax and wane philosophically about fly fishing, but I won't bore you with a bunch of gibberish. I have long known that, other than a few minor skills here and there, fishing, for the most part, is 10 percent skill and 90 percent luck. It's a mystery that will never be solved, and if you can't let it go, it will drive you insane. On the other hand, I am willing to concede that some fishermen are just luckier than other fishermen, but in the end, it's not possible to catch a twenty-pound Atlantic salmon sitting on the couch.

I want to tell you the fishing improved, but it didn't. I had one take and caught one fish the entire week. Joe never managed to get a fish to take, even though it never stopped him from trying. After all, it only takes one good fish to change your disposition. Anadromous fish are what they are. They migrate up the Gaspé rivers to spawn, and from what fisheries biologists tell us, they don't feed once they enter the river. I think that's a bunch of codswallop. Although I do think your chances are much better when the fish first enter the river. The longer the salmon are in the river, the less chance you have of actually catching one. If the conditions improve, you might even get another run of fresh fish, but I wouldn't count on it.

That's one reason why May, June, and July are so expensive. Not only are the fish fresh from the salt, but they also haven't been fished over that heavily. By the time you reach what we call in the South the dog days of summer—August and September—it becomes a crapshoot at best. I have heard the locals call it frog water. During those months, I can only assume you have a better chance of catching a largemouth bass than an Atlantic salmon, or in the case of the Miramichi, probably a smallmouth bass.

The river starts to drop, and the water temperatures begin to climb, and the fish hunker down and wait until the river rises so they can make their way up to Cascapedia Lake and eventually spawn in the spring. Depending on the conditions and the disposition of the salmon, you may or may not be part of the equation. Then again, that's why Atlantic salmon fishing is so addictive. It's challenging and unpredictable in the best of times. Success and failure lie somewhere between your ears, not necessarily in the river.

Why Should British Columbia Be Any Different?

Thomas Wolfe once wrote: "Some things will never change. Some things will always be the same. Lean down your ear upon the earth and listen."

Unlike our trek north, full of hope and early morning promise, our trip south was a little muted, maybe even a bit melancholy at times. In the end, it's just a game, and depending on your expectations, "it's a game that can't be won—only played," at least in the immortal words of Bagger Vance.

By this time, we needed desperately to find a wonderful mom-and-pop diner and a healthy stack of pancakes and bacon to cheer things up. It was time to move on and shift our attention to the Great Northwest. In only a few months, Joe and I would be swinging flies the size of small squid to winter steelhead. At least that was the plan.

Anyone who's ever fished with a guide knows they tend to exaggerate. I could say they flat-out lie at times, but that's a little harsh. However, one could argue that it's closer to the truth than a lie. When it comes to steelhead and British Columbia, fishermen tend to believe every word that comes out of their guide's mouth. It makes perfect sense. You probably have a king's ransom invested in the trip, and the guide is the only thing standing between you and your sanity. Essentially the guides are merely parroting the propaganda coming out of the lodge.

Occasionally someone at the local fly shop might slip up and declare the steelhead fishing is a little off this year. That's about as negative as it gets. So when the lodge owner, the local fly shop manager, and the guides declare in unison that this is the worst year they've seen in the last fifty years, you tend to believe them. Why? Because the same people told you the previous year that it was the best year anyone could remember in the last fifty years, and it was true. Then you convince yourself that it only takes one good steelhead to justify the cost of the trip, especially if it's a twenty-plus-pound steely. The fact that you hadn't seen a twenty-pound fish in the system in years has very little to do with anything. It's been my experience that the lodge rarely, if ever, gives your money back, so there is nothing left to do but go fishing and hope for the best. And that's precisely what we did.

What's the worst that could happen? You spend a few days in a palatial hotel in the Vancouver Airport? You splurge and have dinner in Vancouver at some of the best seafood restaurants on the planet, or peruse some of the best used bookstores in North America? If nothing else you could take in a hockey game after dinner—the choices are endless, and you haven't even made it to the lodge yet. The trip to Vancouver alone is worth the price of admission, and who knows, you might still catch a twenty-pound steelhead. If not, you still get to spend a few days in Vancouver on the way out. I know, I feel your pain; life can be tough at times.

I usually like to keep my customers on a short leash. I am not a control freak by any stretch of the imagination, but I like to know where everyone is at any given time, if not for their safety then for my sanity. Several months before the Far West Frontier Steelhead Lodge trip, Joe Hovious and Gary Whipple, another dyed-in-the-wool steelhead junkie, decided to head up to British Columbia a week early, rent a truck, and do some exploratory fishing on their own. Of course, I wanted to go, but I had to meet two customers flying into Vancouver several days before the trip, and since I own the damn company, I felt it was my responsibility to meet them at the airport and show them around. The majority of my customers are experienced travelers, and the last thing they need is someone babysitting them. But I do have a few customers who always have difficulty navigating some of the land mines that plague the travel industry.

The plan was to meet Steve and Robert at the airport in Vancouver, have dinner and overnight at the Fairmont, then catch an early flight to Smithers the next morning. Hopefully, Joe and Gary would be waiting for us at the airport in Smithers. I am not going to dwell on the previous two days. Suffice it to say, I took an early morning flight out of Mobile, Alabama. I was already checked in and having a hearty bowl of clam chowder and a cold beer in the bar at the Fairmont when the clock struck noon. Steve and Robert decided to take a late-afternoon flight from Atlanta. Little did they know there was a massive cold front working its way east. Unfortunately, Steve and Robert ran smack-dab into the storm and had to make an unscheduled stop in Denver for the night—and that was the good part. (There is no reason to go into a lot of detail here; it wasn't pretty.) The only thing that mattered is they both made it to Smithers on time.

The flight to Smithers is relatively short as the crow flies, and fortunately for us, the weather cooperated. Smithers lies in what could be considered a giant bowl in the middle of a vast mountain range. And late in the year, more often than not it's fogged in or, even worse, snowed in. Of course, if everything went according to plan on a trip, you wouldn't have much to talk about. Let's face it, the trials and tribulations are what make it interesting.

When we finally made it to the lodge, you could feel the tension in the air. It wasn't my first visit to Far West Frontier Steelhead Lodge, but it was the first time that things felt a little off-kilter. Usually the other fishermen are beaming with enthusiasm and you can hardly keep them off the water. To everyone's credit, though, no one seemed to panic. At some fundamental level, experienced steelhead fishermen understand that even under the best of conditions, fly-fishing for winter steelhead is a crapshoot regardless of what you paid for the trip.

There's a vast difference between chasing winter steelhead on your own, or better yet with a handful of close friends, and backing up the Brinks truck to pay for six days of fishing on one of the best steelhead rivers on the planet. Winter steelhead fishing is challenging on so many levels. It's ironic; you probably stand a better-than-even chance of getting skunked regardless of the cost. That's winter steelhead fishing in a nutshell.

The sun fades early in November, and the temperature drops and keeps dropping throughout the night. For someone who grew up in

South Florida it's exhilarating, up to a certain point, then it just feels downright cold. I had three times the clothes on that the other guests were wearing, but by dinnertime the first night, I was down to a pair of jeans and a light pullover. Between the Scotch and the fireplace, I was feeling quite toasty. The walk back to the cabin was a little chilly, but at least I had remembered to turn up the heat before I left for dinner. Between the heater, the flannel sheets, pillowcases, and the two quilts, I slept as if someone had slipped a mickey in my Scotch after dinner.

The next morning, we spent the first hour or so following the twists and turns of an old logging road that snakes its way along the Bulkley and eventually splits off and parallels the Morice. The higher we climbed, the heavier the snow fell. Even with four-wheel drive and tires large enough to float a small battleship, the truck was slipping and sliding from one side of the road to the other. Finally, we pulled off the main road and made our way down to the river. By this time the snow was coming down sideways.

The jet sled was already in the water. All we had to do was clean off all the snow and unload the gear from the truck and drag it down to the boat. The launch was just upriver of where the Morice merges with the Bulkley. It was precisely the same stretch of river where I managed to hook four steelhead on the final day of a trip the previous year. Two of them had come unbuttoned. And if I had to make an educated guess, the two that stayed buttoned was by the grace of some shape-shifting deity. Then again, it could have been a local trickster or possibly a demented transformer—all of which share a prominent role in the local myths and folklore. It's tough to tell which one you're dealing with at any given time. We were on tribal land, and anything was possible. I landed several rather large steelhead that morning. Looking back, it was the perfect ending to a great week of fishing.

Before we pushed off, I told Joe he should have left a few apples and a banana on a paper plate at the base of one of the giant cedars for good luck, but like most of my customers, he probably thinks I'm a little touched. I'm not saying I buy into all the local myths and legends. Still, I have spent enough time on the water with the (Gitxsan) First Nation guides while fishing the Kispiox to know they either truly believe in the local myths and folklore or it's good for business. Regardless of what you think, it's been my experience that a little dose of positive karma never hurt anyone.

When we finally pushed off and made our way upriver, I looked around, expecting to see the same bars and the same troughs I dredged last year. Nut nothing looked familiar. I didn't recognize anything; it was as if I was on a different river altogether. Then it dawned on me that last year the water was lower than anyone could remember in years, and this year the river was running on the high side, in some places over the banks and into the trees.

We usually only fish two to a boat, but today for some reason, Joe, Gary, and I decided to fish together. Unfortunately, this meant that two of us would be alone without a guide or a gun for at least twenty or thirty minutes at a time deep in Grizzly Central. Not that I am afraid of a six- or seven-hundred-pound carnivore with the predisposition of a drunken sailor on a Friday night in Subic Bay after being at sea for the last six months, but for the first hour or the possibility induces an adrenaline rush rarely felt in civilization. The guide dropped Joe off on a great-looking gravel bar upriver from where we launched the boat, and once the guide had set him up and made sure he was comfortable, we took off and pushed upriver. A few minutes later, the guide pulled the sled up on a shallow bar and let me out. He asked me if I was okay. What the hell was I going to say at this point? Then the guide took off before I could ask him for some bear spray or, even better, his fifty caliber and multiple rounds of ammunition.

I stood there and watched the jet sled snake from side to side, fighting the braided current while trying to inch its way upriver. A few seconds later, they took a hard right, weaved in and out of a giant logjam of broken lodgepole pine and fallen cedar, and then faded into the falling snow. The snow always seems to take the edge off everything. It's as if the landscape becomes muted, as if someone turned down the volume. Then it dawned on me that I was truly alone. Maybe that's what we pay for, the opportunity to be alone in a wild landscape and everything else is just the lemon next to the pie. There is more biology to this than meets the eye.

At some fundamental level, this is where it all began. And for some of us, the connection to wild places is really what it's all about.

It didn't take long to realize that if we were going to catch any steelhead, it would take a lot of work, the patience of a Trappist monk, and the dogged determination of a steely-eyed missile man. To make a long story short, I didn't get so much as a tug. Forty-five minutes later, I heard the loud drone of an inboard/outboard jet sled making its way downriver, getting louder the closer it got. I know it sounds a little nerdy, but the first thing I thought about was the Doppler shift. The increasingly loud drone of the jet sled should have sounded out of place on a wild steelhead river like the Morice, but for some reason, it didn't. It almost seemed appropriate at the time. A few minutes later, the jet sled came bouncing around the logjam and picked me up. When it arrived, I was at the tail end of the pool. The water was only inches from the top of my waders. It's a good thing they showed up when they did: I was almost at the point of no return; a slippery rock here and I would have been swimming back to shore. A few minutes later, we picked up Joe. I didn't even ask if he had caught anything or not. Since he didn't seem very excited, I assumed he didn't bump into anything either.

The morning seemed to drag on—swing after swing without so much as a bump, much less a solid tug. It was cold and getting colder by the minute. Fortunately for the four of us, we were wearing several thousand dollars' worth of high-tech winter clothing. Other than a few exposed parts here and there, we stayed rather toasty. There was no reason to fret; we knew the guide carried a tremendous amount of firewood and the kitchen staff had prepared a lunch fit for royalty. We had thermoses full of hot soup, hot chili, hot chocolate, and hot coffee, not to mention dozens of homemade cookies and a multitude of desserts.

Several hours later, we pulled the sled up on what looked like a promising gravel bar, and while the boys and I worked our way down the run, the guide dragged out what looked like half of cord of firewood and a few dead limbs from the nearby deadfall that lined the river. Then he opened a gas can and splashed the firewood with what must have been half a gallon of gasoline. When the guide threw the match on the pile of wet wood, we could hear the initial whoosh sixty or seventy yards downriver. A few minutes later, the fire looked like a towering inferno.

About this time, we packed it in and made our way back to the fire. There are few things in life better than a raging campfire on the banks of a pristine steelhead river in the dead of winter. As far as I was concerned, we could spend the remainder of the day sitting around the campfire. After all, we had only begun to explore this pool and the tailout. Then out of nowhere, Joe pulled out his cell phone and showed us a photo of a hefty steelhead he had caught earlier that morning. He never said a word about catching a fish. The photo was impressive, but the fact he managed to land the fish and take a great photo by himself was even more impressive.

The guide kept digging through the cooler trying to find everyone's lunch, and when he finally handed me a sandwich he mumbled something about our location. I didn't realize it at the time, but this was the same run Joe and I had fished the previous year—and did fairly well, if I remember correctly. Lunch came and went without much fanfare. The guide kept dragging firewood up and down the beach as if he planned to build a log cabin on the banks of the Morice. It didn't make much difference to us where we fished that day. We had a long run with a beautiful tailout in walking distance from the fire. I didn't see any reason to dash off in hopes of a better location. I wasn't sure I wanted to get up at all; I was more than comfortable where I was sitting. Joe and Gary had just managed to make their way back to the river when a drone buzzed us out of nowhere.

Then we noticed some rustling in the woods, and sure enough, two or three engineers came dragging their sorry ass out of the woods with laptops and remote controls for the drone. They were mapping the Morice for the new Coastal GasLink pipeline that would run parallel to the river and eventually cross the Morice somewhere upriver. Of course, the First Nations people and almost every environmentalist and environmental organization on the West Coast opposed the new pipeline. Strangely enough, Oliver, our guide, didn't seem to have much to say about the new pipeline. When pressed, he freely admitted that it was going to create a tremendous number of new jobs, and that he wasn't opposed to the pipeline if it was done right. It would take me some time to come to terms with his response. It was most certainly not the answer I expected.

The insanity of the drone didn't creep in until later that evening. Looking back, I would have given a small fortune for a Holland & Holland side-by-side twelve gauge and blown the piece of shit out of the air. Forty years ago, I probably would have buried the lot in a deep hole somewhere in a dark holler where they would never be found.

The idea that fishermen can pay as much as seven or eight thousand dollars for a week of steelhead fishing and be exposed to such bullshit as the drone boggles the imagination. It seemed even more dramatic because even though the fishing was good, the catching was on the poor side. The river was a little high, which was expected because of all the rain and snow. Other than that, it was in great shape. At some point, though, we had to acknowledge that there wasn't a lot of steelhead in the river.

Other than standing in the river six or seven hours a day swinging flies, the lunches could have easily been considered the highlight of the trip. I'm not complaining; we knew it would be slow, but we never anticipated it would be quite this slow. We had to face reality: We were spoiled after the incredible trip the previous year.

By this time, Joe and Gary had started their slow, methodical march down the river, one step at a time. Cast and step, cast and step, and then out of nowhere Gary's spey reel started screaming "Welcome Back My Friends to the Show That Never Ends," better known as "Karn Evil 9," by Emersion, Lake, and Palmer. Gary was into a good fish. It was all he could do to hang on. Ten or fifteen minutes later, the guide finally managed to slip the net under the fish. We took a few photos and released her quickly.

The days seemed to meld into one; even now, looking back, I can't parse the individual days. I can only remember bits and pieces of the trip. I have to keep reminding myself that there is no such thing as a bad fishing trip. It's just some trips are better than others.

Rarely, if ever, do I get to spend more than three or four weeks a year chasing steelhead. Unlike Atlantic salmon, you can fish for steelhead pretty much year-round if you have the resources and the free time. There is something special about anadromous species. Fly-fishing for steelhead is addicting on so many levels. The anticipation alone has driven fishermen to the bottle. Of course, a flask filled with your favorite beverage works well, though it has been my experience that mixing alcohol and freezing temperatures only works for a few minutes. Then you're cold again, if not freezing. We could fish the Skeena drainage much earlier in the season, and we often do, but for the most part, in late October through November into early December, the Bulkley and Morice Rivers can be breathtaking. And by that time, the rivers are relatively devoid of fishermen.

Each season is entirely different, but winter steelhead fishing borders on some sort of dementia not yet defined by the medical community. For some reason, here we are again. Like last year, the year before that, and the year before that. In some ways, winter steelhead fishing is like self-flagellation. Other times, it's like a juicy rationalization, and once you have come to terms with the absurdity of standing in a freezing river swinging a fly in front of a species that supposedly doesn't feed once it starts its migration up the river, it all starts to make sense. You're just crazy. Either that or you don't have anything better to do with your time.

Looking back, given the right equipment and enough food, I could have spent the next several weeks exploring the upper reaches of the Morice. I have always wanted to blow off a day of fishing and make the run up to Morice Lake. Several guides that I have a lot of respect for have told me that steelhead fishing can be great on the other side of the lake in early winter. From what I can make out using a topographic map, there seems to be dozens of small rivers and tributaries flowing into Morice Lake. That's what fly fishermen do: We stand waist-deep in one of the best steelhead rivers on the planet, and all we can think about is what's around the next bend, the next tributary, the next lake, and so on.

It's amazing what you think about when you're standing in the river. Winter steelhead fishing often gives you time to put life into perspective. It's a respite from the daily grind. For most people, it's a time to dwell on the mortality of all living things: the landscape, the animals, the river itself, and where you fit in. Like all living things, the river is a living, breathing entity that's constantly changing.

The week came and went at the pace of a slug on a cold winter day. There was just enough fish caught that week to prevent the other fishermen from giving up steelheading completely. But the truth is, next year could be one of the best years in the last fifty years. Then again, it could be the worst year in the last fifty years. Or it could be a multitude of variations on the theme. One never knows about such things.

The next morning, we boarded a new Dash 8-Q400 that seated seventy-eight passengers. The old Dash 8-300 only seated fifty-four passengers and was always overbooked, and it was questionable if your luggage would arrive on the same flight. Smithers is deep in the heart of logging country, and between the timber industry and the mining industry, fishermen and their luggage tend to be the least of Air Canada's concerns.

Later that day, we checked into the Fairmont. And after we stowed our luggage and cleaned up a little, we hopped on the subway and headed to Vancouver for dinner. Afterward, Joe and Gary made their way back to the Fairmont. With little else to do, Steve and I spent half the night rummaging through the mom-and-pop bookstores that line the city's back streets and the phenomenal coffee shops and microbreweries that seem to be the cornerstone of Vancouver these days. The next morning the four of us made our way through security and met for a long, leisurely breakfast before we all went our separate ways.

Bodacious Margaritas, Horny Monkeys, and Naked Iguanas

THE SMALL COMMUTER PLANE LANDED RATHER ABRUPTLY ON AMBER-gris Caye on an airstrip that seemed even smaller than the plane. Thankfully, it had been a mercifully short flight from Belize City. The sky was dark, and the winds were howling as the small aircraft bounced its way up and down the runway. Visibility was limited, and I could only assume the pilot wanted to live as much as we did. It reminded me of an F-18 trying to land on a carrier in a strong crosswind in heavy seas.

Sometimes life requires nothing more than a leap of blind faith. Everyone took a deep breath as the small plane came to a screeching halt only a few feet short of the end of the runway. The only passengers on the flight who seemed to be enjoying themselves were the two kids sitting directly in front of me. They were having the time of their life, even though their parents looked a little green around the gills. A few minutes later, we were milling around our luggage. We were trying to figure out the best way to get to the hotel. I finally broke down and asked one of the taxi drivers lined up behind the fence, anxiously waiting for our business, to take us to the Sun Breeze Hotel.

Of course, he said yes. I asked him how much he would charge us. He thought for a minute and then replied, "Twenty dollars American." I wondered if the fare was for one person or the entire group. I was tired and agreed to the twenty dollars American regardless. The next thing I knew, the taxi driver was calling a handful of ragtag street kids to help carry our gear. There must have been a dozen young kids; most of them couldn't have been more than ten years old. They could barely pick up the gear until I showed them how to use the rollers. Then they took the luggage and dashed across the street and disappeared down a little alley. I laughed so hard that I almost spit up the beer I was drinking, but my clients were panicking and soon took chase.

By this time, I had been flying in and out of these small Central American countries for so long that chaos seemed more like the norm than the exception. Panhandlers, fake taxis, pickpockets, you name it, I think I have seen almost everything you could throw at a bunch of happy-go-lucky tourists. I finally decided to follow, though for some reason I didn't think they were stealing the bags, but to be honest, I wasn't totally convinced they weren't either. I crossed the street and ducked into the alley, and as soon as I stepped into the dark corridor, the kids were lined up at the reservation desk at the Sun Breeze Hotel.

The damn hotel was only fifty or sixty feet from the tarmac. We had been taken to the cleaners, even though I thought it was hilarious at the time. I still do. I could only smile and cough up the twenty dollars. In the end, the kids made out like bandits. Everyone felt sorry for them and tipped way over and beyond the call of duty. They tipped the kids so well we couldn't get rid of them! It seemed as if we adopted them for the next three days. We fed them at least once a day and sometimes two or three times a day. We had several ladies in the group, and I think, given the opportunity, they would have adopted the kids. The weather was so bad I spent the next three days teaching some of the older kids how to fly fish. I eventually found out that a fly rod was never going to replace their Cuban yo-yos. Before we left, the kids had new tennis shoes and most of them were dressed exponentially better than they were when we arrived.

Unfortunately, the first three days were proof that when you visit a place for a very short time, you have to be prepared to make the best of whatever conditions you encounter. In our case, the first three days were spent hunkering down from the gale-force winds that were pounding Ambergris Caye. The winds made the fishing all but impossible. We did what we had to do in order to make the best of a poor situation. Weather always plays a part in fishing, and basically there is little you can do about it. Regardless of how badly the wind howled, we still managed to get out every day and do some fishing. We even caught a few fish. John Freeman took a small permit on the front side of Ambergris Caye. Drew and Tom loaded up on bonefish one morning on the back side.

The truth is, Belize is in the tropics, and the wind is supposed to blow, and blow hard at times. The tropics are the tropics precisely because of the tropical winds and rain. At some point, most fly fishermen come to terms with the wind and move on. It's part of the game. That being said, I must admit the winds were much stronger than normal, and we were relegated to fishing the leeward side of the island. The places we could fish were limited not only by the wind but also by the tides. The days were typically cut short. Usually, we managed to get out somewhere around eight-thirty in the morning, or sometimes a little later depending on the tides. We did see a tremendous number of bonefish and a few permit. The fish were small but not very spooky. The average size of the bonefish we ran into was maybe ten to twelve inches long, and the permit we saw rarely exceeded twelve to fourteen inches at best. That doesn't mean this is a fair representation of the average size of the fish. Possibly, the bigger fish had hunkered down offshore on the ocean side of the reef, waiting for the wind to die down and the dirty water to clear. In any event, it didn't appear that they were particularly interested in coming out to play with a gang of gringos from the States.

We did what most fishermen would do under similar circumstances: We hunkered down, fished when we could, and spent copious amounts of time at the bar learning the local cocktail lingo—Bodacious Margaritas, Horny Monkeys, Naked Iguanas, and rumrunners—while nibbling shrimp on a stick, panfried pot stickers, and other delightful treats. It turns out the Blue Water Bar and Grill is one of the best restaurants and tiki bars on the beach. Somehow, given enough time, things seem to always work out for the best.

The Blue Water Bar and Grill, we learned, is a great place to pass the time and to meet up for a stroll through San Pedro to check out the local culture. A lot of the latter, readily accessible to the short-term tourist, centers on fishing and the fine art of mixology. Thus, for pure anthropological research, Jim Whitehurst and I made it our goal to discover the absolute best bartenders in town. We found them in a spot called the Sunset Grill. In our scientific opinion, which is shared by many, this bar does in fact have the best margaritas in San Pedro. An additional perk is the common ritual of "feeding the tarpon."

The Sunset Grill has a long dock with overhead lights that shine into the water where tarpon gather at night to be fed. The bartenders meet you under the lights with a bucket of pilchards that you are then welcome to hand-feed to the fish. While most tourists might daintily throw the pilchards at the tarpon like so many toy koi, real fly fishermen lie down on the dock and swirl a pilchard on the surface of the water until the tarpon explodes on the bait. If the same crusty old fly fisherman is willing to sacrifice a few layers of epidermis, a little game of "tease the tarpon," which involves pulling the sardine away at the last moment, can be very entertaining. It turns out that after a few repetitions of this trick the tarpon get thoroughly pissed off. Perhaps for some, lying face down a few feet from the water with twenty to thirty tarpon ranging from fifty to seventy pounds that are rolling, crashing, and turning the water into froth, furiously straining to bite off the hand of the ruddy idiot with the pilchard, may not sound like much fun. This sport gets intense! Fingertips can get reduced to sandpaper. For a fisherman, however, this is about as much fun as can be had with tarpon without using a fly rod.

All good things come to an end. All in all, the three days spent in San Pedro chasing after small fish and deep margarita glasses did serve one valuable purpose exceedingly well. The more time we spent in San Pedro, the slower the time seemed to pass, which, in the larger picture, is exactly what is supposed to happen. However, it was time for us to move south and explore the more pristine side of Belize. We didn't know it yet, but we were about to discover the land of plenty. Our destination was South Water Caye and the Blue Marlin Lodge. Of course, by this time I had to convince some of my clients to get back on the plane. Some even considered hitchhiking south at least as far as Dangriga.

We were met at the airport by the Blue Marlin Lodge staff. After a short trip through town toward the owner's home, we were finally taken by boat to the lodge, which is about eight miles south from Dangriga and just north of Placencia. It only took a few minutes into the boat ride to realize we were in a different world down here. The open water was so blue it was almost black. The atoll and the inside flats that run parallel to the coast of Belize can literally be seen from miles away. It was as if the flats glowed in the daylight. The islands were thick with giant mangroves. The water teemed with life, and schools of pilchards were everywhere. Cero mackerel and bonita were slicing through the pilchards, driving them to the surface where the pelicans made an easy meal of them. Giant frigate birds soared above the mayhem, waiting to pounce on the bounty below. Every third island or so we ran past enormous rookeries full of herons, egrets, pelicans, and more frigate birds than you could count. To us, it felt as if we had rediscovered Eden. It quickly became the consensus that we could have skipped northern Belize entirely.

I was on top of the world, disregarding the heart-wrenching realization that we had only three days in this paradise to catch a permit. I knew the time would fly by. Twenty minutes later the thirty-foot center console eased into the dock and we got our first look at the Blue Marlin Lodge, surrounded by white-sand beaches and littered with tall, swaying palm trees. South Water Caye is a beautiful island that stretches south along the world's second-longest atoll.

As we pulled alongside the dock, a large school of bonefish pushed away from the boat. Most lodges have pet fish around the docks. Normally the fish are extremely large, and the lodges rarely let you fish for them. I was teasing Rosella, the owner of the Blue Marlin Lodge, and Richard, the manager, about their pet bonefish. Richard calmly told me to rig my fly rod and hop into one of the pangas tied up to the other side the dock. Minutes later, while everyone else was unpacking, Richard and I pulled away from the dock, and in a very short time I was casting to a school of bonefish in the four- to five-pound range. Proper etiquette might possibly have dictated that I wait for everyone to unpack so they could share in the spoils. I did think about it for approximately a millisecond. After such thorough consideration, I arrived at the conclusion that the others were probably tired from the trip and would much prefer to calmly and orderly unpack their belongings before rushing headlong into another adventure. Additionally, it is very much my duty as trip host to scope out the area before exposing my valued friends to it. So I went fishing and kindly left them in peace. The fish were three times the size of the largest bonefish we had seen in northern Belize. Within the first thirty minutes of fishing South Water Caye and the Blue Marlin Lodge, I had hooked and landed two rather large bonefish.

That night over dinner, the conversation was much more optimistic than it had been in San Pedro. In some cases, it was downright giddy. Everyone was in great spirits, only partially related to the quantity of margaritas being imbibed. Once again, it did occur to me for several nanoseconds that we might conceivably pay gravely for our lack of self-control the following morning. Even with the overindulgence of libations, I managed to muster enough energy to scope out the pier to see if there was any action under the lights. I could only walk so fast; the bar was closing, and at eight dollars a pop for a margarita, I didn't want to spill my drink. However, the closer I got to the lights, the faster I walked, drawn by the sound of small tarpon exploding on the water's surface.

There must have been a dozen small permit laid up in the current and, adding to the embarrassment of riches, schools of bonefish were mudding their way along the bottom a few puffs at a time. I have been fishing for snook and tarpon under the lights of South Florida for over forty years, and I have never yet seen a bonefish or a permit in the lights. I must have been drooling, or at the very least, looked somewhat ridiculous. I felt a combination of dumbfounded excitement, disbelief, and greed.

Several of the guides had followed me down to the pier. To be honest, I didn't realize they were guides at the time, but they looked like guides, they carried themselves like guides, and they drank like guides, so in the immortal words of Cheech and Chong, they must be guides. This was the first time I met my guide, Ivan. It was an instant friendship forged over margaritas and pot stickers and the love of permit. For the next two hours, all we talked about was permit and bonefish. For most of his life, Ivan had been a commercial fisherman and loved it. He became a guide out of necessity. It seems that the Belize government cracked down on the commercial fishermen when they finally concluded that the government made more money off the tourist industry via taxes than what little money they collected through the commercial fishing license program. We stood around laughing and joking about the fish; according to Ivan, there had been several grand slams caught here off the dock and even more slams finished there. He boldly stated that when I caught my permit and bonefish the next day, this is where I would probably finish my slam with a tarpon. I immediately fell in love with Ivan!

I took a long, hard sip of my margarita and then gave it to Ivan and started running to my bungalow to get my gear. At least I intended it to be a run; the speed and elegance of the process suffered from inappropriate footwear. (There's a reason why sprinters don't practice in flip-flops!) Eventually, I made it to my room, doing my best not to wake up my roommate Drew. The young lad needed his rest. I had to turn on the lights to get my fly rod and a box of tarpon flies. When the lights came on, Drew jumped up as if I had just pulled the fire alarm.

He immediately asked where the hell I was going. Too much information can trouble the mind, so I told him I was considering taking a stroll down the pier and maybe pitching a few flies under the lights to see if there were any jacks or ladyfish around. In response, Drew mumbled something to the effect of "yeah right," and before I could make up another cover story to ease his self-sacrificing drive to join me, he was out the door. Rumors filtered through the lodge for the next several days that I had actually tried to trip the poor kid as he went by. If I did, then it was only for his own good, to be sure. Since Drew is a lot younger than me, and he's an avid soccer player on top of it, I doubt I could have caught him in my flip-flops. Somehow I had to stop him. If not, he was going to wake up the entire lodge while trying to get his gear out the door and down the stairs.

As it turned out, I could have saved myself all the effort and politeness. When we finally made it back to the pier, there were people everywhere! It was a small comfort that none of them were fishing "my pier," but there was still too much noise and too many people walking around. Knowing that the best time to fish the lights under a pier is late at night when everything is dead quiet, I was rapidly losing my enthusiasm. I love to catch a tide change somewhere around three or four in the morning. The tide change, mind you, not the shift change. I didn't know it at the time, but there were several smaller lodges on the back side of the island. However, the Blue Marlin Lodge is the only lodge on the island with a restaurant and bar; maybe it is simply the only decent restaurant and bar on the island. Who knows?

We had such a good time at dinner that I failed to notice the additional customers filling up the outside seating on the deck overlooking the water. While I was away retrieving my gear, a few customers couldn't help noticing all the guides milling around the pier and decided to walk down and check out the action. The last thing I wanted to do was hook someone in the head with a fly. I had to accept defeat for the time being, and I put my rod down to wait for the crowd to thin out.

Without any spectacle to keep the onlookers entertained, it took only about an hour or so for the pier to empty, except for a few guides and Drew. Fortunately, the tarpon were still chasing shrimp in the shadows. Unfortunately, the permit and bonefish had long since disappeared. I quickly tied on an EP Mullet imitation and started working the shadow-line off the end of the pier. There were more tarpon under the lights closer to shore, but less noise and fewer people at the end. I jumped a small tarpon on my fifth or sixth cast but immediately lost him. Several minutes later, I had another take but did not get the opportunity to set the hook. I spent the next several hours pounding the water with everything but the deck mop lying in an old panga.

The tarpon never left, but the tide went slack and the shrimp were all but gone. The only bait left around the lights was small schools of pilchards and a few glass minnows. Even though the occasional tarpon would blast one here and there, it was readily apparent they had been there to gorge on the shrimp and not fool around with pilchards. It was time to call it a night. After all this exertion, on my way back to the room, it occurred to me that the real mystery here was whether I would be able to fish for permit eight to ten hours a day in the brutal sun, have dinner, spend some time at the bar, and fish all night at the pier for three straight days. There was a time in my life when this would not have even been a question.

The next day I had several shots at a few big permit without so much as a sniff, and of course, the next night I was back at the pier. The usual suspects were all there; the tarpon was still hammering the shrimp, and there were several bonefish still picking away at the bottom. There was also a lone permit sitting motionless under the lights. I watched for what must have been an hour—in fact, for over an hour. I was staring at a potential grand slam and a good one at that. Right in front of me, within twenty feet, I had a forty- to fifty-pound tarpon, several four- or five-pound bonefish, and the biggest prize of all, a twelve- to thirteen-pound permit. All I was missing was a rod, and the motivation to repeat the previous night's comedy of errors. I finally gave up trying to solve life's little problems and went to bed. The next several days showed promise, but at some point you finally realize that trying to catch a permit on the fly requires a tremendous amount of time and energy and an extraordinary amount of time on the water. I put my hope in Ivan's hands, the martinet schoolmaster. Then again, a little luck goes a long way sometimes.

Permit at Ten O'clock, Sixty Feet Out, and Closing

IT'S ONLY MY HUMBLE OPINION, AND WE ALL KNOW WHAT THAT'S worth (I doubt my opinion and seventy-five cents will buy you a cup of coffee in a cheap diner). But I think the permit deserves its place in the pantheon of gamefish beside the Atlantic salmon and the steelhead. Depending on whether you prefer the gin-clear saltwater flats and estuaries of the tropics or the freshwater rivers of the northern hemisphere, the permit might be at the pinnacle or, depending on your taste, a distant third. I think it's the greatest show on earth. Don't get me wrong. I dearly love steelhead and Atlantic salmon fishing, and especially the environments in which they're found.

I grew up fishing in South Florida and the Florida Keys, and I guess I am nothing more than a product of my environment. I can hear the hordes of tarpon and bone fishermen screaming in the background, "What about the tarpon and bonefish?" I feel your pain, I really do, but in the end, a bonefish is nothing more than a seagoing pilchard for the reef sharks to chase. Although hooking, fighting, and landing a giant tarpon might be one of the most exciting things you can do with your clothes on, it's not the same. A permit on the fly is the ultimate visual experience. From my perspective, nothing even comes close. By hook or crook, permit came into possession of Harry Potter's invisibility cloak somewhere. At the slightest noise or even a subtle sense of danger, they fade away as if they never existed in the first place.

To be a good permit fishermen, you need, at the very least, a masochistic streak. A want ad looking for qualified permit fishermen might read something like this: "Wanted: Permit fishermen. Must be able to cast a fly a minimum of ninety feet into gale-force winds and lay it down softly in an area the size of a saucer. Must be a sadomasochist at heart and be able to travel at a moment's notice. It helps to be single and filthy rich." Okay, I will admit that might be an exaggeration of sorts, but not much of one.

I doubt I will ever forget the moment I realized that trying to catch a permit on the fly is sheer lunacy. I was standing on the deck of a run-down panga, which had obviously been in service for many years and seen its fair share of action. It was day five of a seven-day trip. Time was running out, as we were headed home in a couple of days. Ivan and I had been chasing permit off and on for the last few days without so much as a tug.

I remember with almost perfect clarity the spiritual awakening, the epiphany, the moment I finally realized how ridiculous it was to think I could hoodwink a permit with a twisted piece of steel, two lead eyes wrapped with fluorescent green thread, and few pieces of 1960s shag carpet. Suddenly it occurred to me that I was chasing what's considered to be the spookiest fish in the ocean. A fish with the personality of a paranoid schizophrenic, unrivaled vision, nostrils the size of a large slushy straw, and somehow I expected at least one to swim over and slurp up my fly as if it was just another crab crawling along the bottom. In sober consideration, such expectation borders on dementia, a break from reality, a condition caused by too many days in the hot sun glaring into the abyss. Then again, if I were particularly prone to sober consideration, I wouldn't be trying to catch anything on a damn fly to begin with.

Moments earlier, leading up to this epiphany, we were staked out on the perfect permit flat south of Dangriga and just north of Placencia in central Belize. The flat was crawling with life. Stingrays were blowing off the flat in all directions. Marl crunched under the pressure of our push pole. Conch shells, starfish, and miniature crustaceans littered the flat. Grunts and small yellowtails were also in almost unseemly abundance. I remember joking with Ivan about it. I might have mentioned something about fried grunts with grits, or maybe it was yellowtail stuffed with shrimp and scallops, smothered in a creamy champagne sauce. Knowing me, it was probably grunts and grits with a side of hushpuppies and a cold beer, or maybe sweet tea. The truth of the matter is it was difficult to concentrate on grunts and grits when our focus was squarely on the permit, slowly tailing their way up the flat.

It was an easy cast. The wind was at my back. By this time, Ivan had spun the panga around, so the sun and the wind were at the proper angle. All was good in the world. The pressure was off. Hard-earned personal experience had by then convinced me that it was, in fact, utterly impossible to catch a permit on the fly. Unless perhaps one of them was kind enough to contemplate the broader meaning and intrinsic value of a near-death experience just at the opportune moment and for that reason decide to cooperate. I wasn't counting on it. Thus, casting to a school of twenty or so permit in the seventeen- to twenty-pound range had been reduced to the same analytical thrill as casting to Hula-Hoops in the backyard: blasé, routine, ho-hum. I was over the hype, convinced it couldn't be done, at least not intentionally.

I made the cast. The fly hit the lead permit on the head, exactly where the so-called experts tell you to put it. However, being hit with something in the head does not induce a permit to eat; instead, it appeared to have startled him. Long story short, the school exploded in all directions. Ivan almost fell off the poling platform. Incredulous, the two of us stood there for a few moments staring after the spooked fish, both equally stunned and disgusted. It was amazing just how quiet it had become, as if neither of us wanted to so much as take a breath.

It's been my experience that a good fly fisherman either lives in the moment or never learns, depending on your perspective. As we watched, the permit started regrouping several hundred yards down the flat's leeward side. Time to try again! From our vantage point, all we could see was a dozen or so black tails glistening in the bright sun. It was enough to make your heart go pitter-patter. Stealthily, Ivan pushed the heavy panga against the wind with everything he could muster. For me to get a worthwhile cast, Ivan had to position the panga so that my back was against the mangroves. Between the mangroves, the wind, and the distance to the permit, this effort could rationally have been judged as futile, if not ludicrous. Immune to such nonconstructive truths, I made what I thought at the time to be an exceptionally lousy cast. The fly hit the water with the subtlety of a ground-to-air missile. I only missed by forty or so feet—nothing like adding a little humiliation to spice up the day! Ivan looked at me as if to say, "Really, that's the best you can do?"

I started to pick the line up off the water to make another cast when Ivan began yelling from the poling platform, "Let the fly drop, let it drop."

Soon it was, "Let the freaking fly drop," so I did.

Incredibly, the permit started moving toward my fly. Several seconds later, they were circling my Merkin Crab, tailing and flashing as if they were going to eat it this time. Slowly, I stripped it along the bottom, painfully, inch by inch. Looking back, if I had it to do all over, I would have let the Merkin sit on the bottom and let the current do all the work. The permit continued harassing my fly all the way to the boat. It seemed they were so focused on the fly that they were oblivious to the panga. So close were they in the end that I could have reached down and tailed a free-swimming permit with my bare hands. Which, in retrospect, I stood a better chance of doing than hooking one with the fly.

A few hours later, the day ended once again without any permit. As always, I kept telling myself that it's the chase that counts. Of course, that logic only goes so far. At some point in time, you have to hook a permit, right? Holding firmly to the ancient wisdom of the frequently unsuccessful but always tenacious fly fisherman, Ivan and I joined the evening celebration of good food and wine shared with great friends, followed by some late-night drinks at the bar. This night was a little different; there was actually a cause for celebration. It turned out that Jim Whitehurst had been fishing a few flats farther down from our location and had managed to hook and land a beautiful double-digit permit. News like that tends to make you reevaluate your previous, perhaps somewhat hasty, nomination of "great friends."

Ivan and I looked at each other in disbelief, wondering what kind of heartless friend catches a permit on the fly when the rest of his friends have determined that the very idea is impossible? Then again, his success meant it could be done, which was all the more reason to go back and try again the next day. On the other hand, drowning your sorrows in a few early-morning rumrunners and crawling back into bed wasn't off the table either. They both had their upsides.

I can't tell you how many times I've been asked why we do this to ourselves over and over again. In the end, it comes down to the thrill of the challenge, the insuppressible conviction that the next cast is going to be "the one."

As a consolation prize, there is always the companionship of friends, great food, late-afternoon cocktails, warm weather, and a beautiful setting to ease the pain—with the emphasis on late-afternoon cocktails. Even though we all know that's nothing more than a juicy rationalization to cope with the pain of not hooking, much less catching, a permit on the fly.

Maybe somewhat unfortunately for my old bones, but absolutely in keeping with my childlike enthusiasm, Ivan and I got an early start the next day. We headed north toward Dangriga while all the other boats headed south toward Placencia. Over the years, I have learned to have faith in my guide until he persuades me otherwise. With Ivan, it was insurmountable faith. He is undoubtedly one of the best permit guides I've ever had the pleasure to share a panga with, hands down.

We were soon running hard up the leeward side of most of the small islands and reefs, trying to put some distance between the lodge and us. I find it difficult to describe the feeling I get when zigzagging in and out of the mangrove islands and skimming over the shallow-water flats at high speeds in the early morning. The sun still sits low in the east, and temperatures are comparatively cool. The towering mangroves break up the sun's rays across the shallow flats, and then one of the most incredible ecosystems on the planet comes alive. It's almost a religious experience! It finally dawned on me what Larry Darrell must have felt like in *The Razor's Edge* as the sun came up and fragmented over the horizon. The answer is never the same for any two people, but rarely does it have anything to do with fishing. Some people call it the magic hour. I think it is as close to Heaven as I can get and still have my feet firmly attached to a little piece of terra firma.

In the morning, the tide was still dropping, and we had several hours to kill before the flats and shallow reefs would start to flood. In this part of the world, the early flood signals "permit time."

Most guides worth their salt have a few out-of-the-way places where there's a good chance of running into a few permit even before the flood tide. Ivan was no exception. He is also the type of guide who despises staying in any one place very long. For the next several hours, we cruised from one flat to another, looking for tailing fish. We were always on the lookout for mudding rays and their happy little companions.

When the tide started to change, we were anchored up on what the locals call the Shark Hole. In reality, it was a mini blue hole. The Shark Hole was a round depression in the middle of an open flat that dropped off to somewhere around a hundred feet. Most blue holes were formed shortly after the last ice age. As the sea level rose, existing sinkholes and caves begin to fill with seawater. We anchored and drifted back with the tide, stopping at the edge, which dropped straight down. One minute the water could be waist-deep, and the next minute the water was so deep a person could disappear without anyone ever knowing what happened. Almost immediately, the permit started to rise from the depths. There were hundreds of them. Ivan told me, "This is where I bring my customers when nothing else works."

While this was obviously intended as nice words of comfort, it felt like a knife penetrating my back. Why would he tell me that? It was like telling a football team getting ready to play its second game of the season: "If we do not win this one, boys, the season's over."

What happens if the team loses the game? Where do you go from there, home? Not that I am trying to shift blame here; that would be counter to my moral character. Obviously, we know what happened in the end. If the reader feels compelled to blame poor Ivan and his loose mouth, what can I possibly do to dissuade? In any event, the morning was passing quickly, and we headed off to a new flat. It was almost time to start contemplating lunch when we rounded the corner of an extensive mangrove island. As we were sliding across the skinny water, we heard someone screaming from the mangroves. I had no idea what he was saying and even less of a notion where he was. I couldn't see anyone, let alone a boat. The next thing I knew, Ivan was slowing down and heading for an opening in the mangroves. I can remember looking back at Ivan and wondering, "Do we really want to do this?"

I had no idea who was in the mangroves, how long he had been there, or what he wanted with us. Sure, we weren't boating off the coast of Somalia, but my natural curiosity to find out what was around the next bend was nonetheless somewhat tempered. Unimpressed by my hesitancy, Ivan pulled in anyway. To my surprise, there was John Freeman, sacked out on the deck of a panga. The person who had been yelling from the mangroves turned out to be Ivan's nephew, another guide from the lodge. He had pulled into the mangroves to get out of the sun and have some lunch. It seemed like a great idea, so we joined in.

After lunch, Ivan and I pushed even farther north in search of a permit. Ivan was moving faster than any guide I had ever fished with. He seemed to be a man possessed. He pushed so hard and so far north, we probably could have spent the night at Turneffe Flats. Ivan and I had rehashed my varied and universally gut-wrenching permit experiences at lunch. I know he wanted to be the guide that put me on my first permit on a fly. Thus, after passing up what I considered to be far too many good-looking permit flats, he took a hard turn starboard and throttled back just in time to come off plane, sliding into a small channel separating two beautiful flats. The bottom was perfect: sand, hard marl, and an abundance of mangroves everywhere. There was plenty of deep water on both sides of the flats for an easy escape, and best of all, there were tails, lots of permit tails!

I did what I do best when I'm permit fishing. I cast to twenty or so fish over the next hour. And for my patience and skill, I experienced every imaginable form of refusal. I spooked fish; I had fish follow my fly, then spook; I had a fish flare at my fly, then spook; I had permit follow my fly back to the boat, and then just swim away with disdain. Every time I looked back at Ivan for some spiritual insight, he just laughed. Ivan kept telling me we had plenty of time to catch a permit, but I knew differently. The clock was ticking. I had been down this dark and dusty road before. Sure, there were two and a half days of fishing left on the calendar, but in reality there were only about fourteen good hours of tide left. The internal clock can drive you mad! It's as if time ebbs away with the tide, and all that's left is a giant hole in my stomach and the stark realization that I blew it again.

Having watched me struggle in one place long enough, Ivan was about to pole off the flat when we spooked a rather large permit mudding. The permit beat feet for open water, and seconds before he crossed the threshold into the deep water, I laid one across his bow. The fly landed directly in front of him. I did not give it much of a chance because my fly line was literally lying across the permit's back. Typically, that is enough to send a permit into orbit, but the fish had been feeding when we spooked him, and that made all the difference. The permit went tail up and descended to the bottom to check out my fly. Ivan started screaming, "Leave it alone, leave it alone, strip it, leave it alone."

I looked back and asked Ivan to please make up his mind. The fish was hot. Ivan went from barking out orders about the retrieve to hollering, "Set the hook, set the hook, set the hook!" This time in Spanglish for additional effect.

I returned volley with, "He doesn't have it, he doesn't have it," though not in Spanglish. Ivan, however, insisted, "He's got to have it."

I continued with my determined denial, "I'm telling you, he doesn't have it."

Meanwhile, I was stripping the fly slowly across the bottom and eventually got to the point where I knew the fish would see the boat and bolt for deep water. Sure enough, that is precisely what happened. Again, I put one across his bow, and the permit reacted in exactly the same manner. We repeated the game one more time for good measure. The permit never ate the fly. It seemed to me the permit was very likely only out for a little afternoon fun, and I happened to be the only game in town. A permit can have a wicked sense of humor. After the permit finally disappeared, I grabbed a couple of beers from the cooler and sat down. The clock was ticking, and this day was in the books. We buttoned down the hatches and settled in for the long ride back to the lodge.

The next morning, we woke to heavy rains and howling winds blowing out of the northeast. Not exactly what I would call ideal fishing conditions. To his credit, although the rains would eventually stop, the winds didn't seem to deter Ivan's enthusiasm in the least. We loaded the boat and pushed south with the wind, knowing damn well that if the wind did not lie down in the afternoon, the ride home would be brutal if not a little dangerous. I knew running directly into a thirty-mile-an-hour wind was out of the question, quite mad actually, but I couldn't get the image of all the permit tails we saw the previous day out of my head. I have to admit, the little kid in me really wanted to go north. My God, I love this game!

Despite the fact we had the wind at our back, it was a wet, slow, and very bumpy ride south. To make things worse, we had an additional hour to waste because the tides normally run on average an hour later every day. Regardless of the time of the day, the tide changes might guarantee an additional hour on the back side. It does not necessarily guarantee an additional hour of good fishing conditions. Two hours before a dead low tide is not necessarily any better than an hour before a dead low. In most cases, it just means you have a little more water to fish.

The topography south of South Water Caye is basically the same as the north and at times just as fishy, but there is considerably more wading available along the inside of the reefs that stretch along the southern coastline. Ivan rarely felt the need to leave the panga. It goes against his core belief of hit and run and cover as much ground as possible on the incoming tide. After only three days of fishing together, Ivan had become my version of Hemingway's Santiago, but poling a twenty-three-foot panga in a thirty-mile-an-hour wind was even a little too much for the great Ivan. We needed to regroup and develop a new game plan. To my surprise, we went even farther south.

We had an early lunch to maximize our time and spend more of it fishing the rising tide. We knew it was going to be a long run home tonight, and that we would be pulling into the docks long after dinner. Neither one of us cared too much about that; after all, we knew the bar would be open late. The modus operandi entailed running south to where Ivan knew of two or three expansive flats that paralleled the reef. It would require wading over the hard, uneven coral bottom for the remainder of the day. It seemed like a small price to pay at the time.

We arrived at the first location, and then cruised up and down the outside of the flat, hoping to see some telltale signs of permit. It was hard to see anything with all the whitecaps, let alone permit tailing. Ivan ran upwind and up current of the flat and anchored the panga securely. We hopped out and started wading south along the reef. The reefs were wide here, and the trick is to split up, one on the inside and one as close as possible to the break. This is where it gets tricky because the water gets deeper and the waves get bigger. The closer to the break, the bigger the coral gets. Large clusters of brain coral and giant families of fan coral littered the bottom. Then the realization dawns on you: If you happen to see a permit, much less hook one, how in hell could you ever land it?

The day turned out to be physically brutal. We walked and waded for seven or eight hours. I tripped, fell, and occasionally went for a quick swim, which was very refreshing and purely intentional of course. In truth, it was not quite as bad as it sounds; we did see a tremendous number of permit that day. The problem was getting into position to make a cast. When fish were spotted, they were either cruising or tailing and seemed to be going in the wrong direction. To get close enough to make a decent cast meant working your way around the permit to get ahead of them. Even though the wind and waves were brutal, it did give me an advantage. I knew if I could get in front of the permit, I could get unbelievably close to the fish without being detected. On several occasions, I managed to get almost too tight. In one case, Ivan and I were down on our knees as I tried to make a sidearm cast to a school that had to number in the twenties. The problem was I did not have any fly line left. My twelve-foot leader was already through the tip of the rod. Seconds later, the school exploded around our feet. I have never been that close to so many angry permit; it was breathtaking!

All we could do was laugh and move on. We pushed the envelope that day, as much as we could. There were still several hours of good fishable tide left, but the sun was getting very low in the west. If we pushed any farther, we might risk making the long run back in the dark. Pangas, unfortunately, are most definitely not set up to run at night, especially not in rough conditions. That being said, Ivan and I were nothing short of determined and adventurous. It was a toss-up. We could stay and fish at the risk of making the long run in the dark or play it safe and head back to the lodge. We came to a quick compromise: We would run as fast as possible without sinking the panga, then slow down and check out the flats we had fished on the way down. If we could see any permit, we would stop and fish them. Let the chips fall where they may. In the end, we slowed down a few times, but the late-afternoon sun made it all but impossible to see tailing fish, especially at any distance.

We managed to make it back to the lodge in plenty of time for dinner. I even had time for a cocktail before dinner, always comforting to the soul, especially when imbibed in the prone position on a beautiful, white-sand beach in the tropics. After dinner, Ivan and I were rehashing the day's events over two of the best margaritas I've ever tasted. Both of us share the opinion that we should have stayed and fished when we had the chance.

Surly Cameramen, Permit, and the Occasional Hurricane

SOMETIMES LIFE SEEMS TO FALL IN PLACE. THE PLANET, THE STARS, AND the universe all align in galactic bliss, and you realize that life might not be all that bad after all! When it happens on a permit flat, it can be downright righteous. It only feels that way because it rarely happens, at least not enough to call it intentional. Then again, it probably happens more times than you might expect because you spend a tremendous amount of time on the water. You finally have some fundamental understanding of the tides. Before you know it, you begin to understand the relationship between the tides, the permit, and the moon. It finally dawns on you that permit by nature are nocturnal creatures, and if you're fishing on a full moon, the odds of catching a permit in the daytime is significantly reduced.

Finally, you have an epiphany. You start picking your dates more carefully. You avoid the spawning season because, depending on where you fish, permit spawn offshore in deeper water more often than not. You catch a few permit now and then, and eventually word gets out, and the next thing you know, customers start calling you asking for advice. Before long, you're the latest Johnny-come-lately so-called permit expert, which you are most certainly not! Then it gets worse. Chris Pipes, the marketing manager for Deep Water Cay, calls you up one day and wants you to give a presentation on fly-fishing for permit to the West Palm Beach Fishing Club, the second-oldest fishing club in the world. Other than the International Game Fish Association in Dania, Florida, it's the most respected sport fishing institution on the planet. Could it get worse? Of course it could! I was expected to share this seminar with Razz Reid, one of the best permit fishermen on the planet. It's incredible how fast that perfect universe can unravel!

The day finally arrived. I drove over to Amelia Island and spent the night with Chris and his wife, Liz. The next morning Chris and I hit the road early to avoid as much morning traffic as possible. That's an illusion of sorts. It's something we tell ourselves so we don't show up depressed. Essentially these days, Florida's east coast is nothing more than one long string of humanity that starts just north of Jacksonville and terminates in Key West. It's nothing more than a walking, talking, breathing organism, something akin to a giant tapeworm. There is no escaping it. Unfortunately, it's only getting worse. I was headed to a part of the world I grew up in. I had done my best to avoid Dade, Broward, and Palm Beach Counties like the plague. I didn't want to be continuously reminded that the world I grew up in was gone and will never be the same again.

Regardless of how much I tried to play it down, I admit I was getting excited! That is, until we pulled off the turnpike in Palm Beach. The traffic was choked like an overgrown algae-filled septic tank. Surrounded by New York, New Jersey, and Massachusetts's license plates, I felt like a tourist. I had to keep reminding myself this was supposed to be fun. After all, it was a privilege to be invited to the Palm Beach Fishing Club. The list of great fishermen who had either presented at or belonged to the PBFC reads like the hall of fame for great fishermen, artists, and writers. The walls are littered with plaques and trophies, representing a multitude of world records by club members. I would be standing in practically the same spot as Lefty Kreh, A. J. McClane, Stu Apte, Flip Pallot, and other great fishermen who once addressed the members of the PBFC. Was I nervous? Not really, well . . . maybe in the first few minutes, but I soon overcame the stress and moved on. Perhaps it was because most of the audience was wearing flip-flops, shorts, and some type of fishing shirt. There were a half dozen or so Miami Dolphin T-shirts and baseball caps in the crowd. It was strange. For some reason, I felt like I was home. This is where I belonged.

Halfway through the presentation, the inevitable happened. A gentleman in the front row raised his hand and asked me how many permit I had caught in my lifetime.

I asked him, "Do you mean using live crabs and live shrimp or exclusively flies?"

And of course, he said, "Flies."

I looked at Razz Reid, and he just smiled, then I turned to the crowd and proudly told the gentlemen in the front row that I had caught thirteen permit on the fly and probably lost three times that many. Over the last twenty-five years, I had probably cast to hundreds of permit. I have experienced every kind of refusal you could dream of, not to mention dozens of ways you couldn't dream of! On the other hand, I had caught at least eighty or so permit on live crabs and shrimp, and rarely spooked any. You can read anything into that you want to.

The next question out of his mouth was, "How long have you been fishing for permit?"

There is always one in every crowd, and it's their sole responsibility to embarrass the speaker. Sometimes you can pick them out, and other times they lie in wait to ambush you by asking stupid questions. Of course, they already know the answer, or they wouldn't have asked the question in the first place. It's not knowledge they're looking for, it's recognition. I was just the latest patsy to respond to his questions.

I answered, "Twenty-five intentionally."

Then, with a sort of snarky attitude, he asked me, "How much time do you spend on the water?"

I politely replied, "Give or take, two hundred and fifty days a year, but not all of it is spent chasing permit."

I should have never gone down this road in the first place. I didn't really care who this guy was. All I wanted to do was shut him up and quickly move on. But I didn't. I continued, "I spend a great deal of time chasing steelhead on the West Coast, Atlantic salmon across the Arctic Circle, and sea-run browns in Patagonia. I spend just as much time chasing tarpon and bonefish throughout the Bahamas and the Caribbean.

If I have any free time left over, I try to the fish the west coast of Costa Rica and chase sailfish and roosterfish on the fly. And if I'm lucky and the rains don't come early, I cross the central ridge and drop down to Manzanillo and chase giant tarpon at the mouth of the Sixaola River."

He just smiled and said, "I'm impressed!"

At that point I piled it on. "The Sixaola River is essentially the southern border between Costa Rica and Panama. It's one of the last clear-water tarpon fisheries left in Central America. It's a seldom-fished resource except for the locals, who much prefer lobsters and crabs to tarpon. Essentially, it's the second coming of Homosassa."

Then he mentioned something about carrying my luggage. I picked up where I had left off and finished my presentation. The crowd was great! Then it was Razz Reid's turn. This was unfair on so many levels. Razz had been a member of the PBFC for many years and knew everyone, and he was on a first-name basis with most of the crowd. Everyone knew of his reputation and the number of permit he had caught throughout the years.

I paid attention to every word that came out of his mouth. Why not listen? Razz had a lifetime of experience chasing permit. Only a fool would ignore him. We had known each other for many years. A few months earlier, Razz and I were sitting in Dreamland Barbecue in Mobile, Alabama, enjoying plate after plate of barbecue ribs, pulled pork sandwiches, and sweet tea. We were discussing Atlantic salmon fishing and the Gaspé.

Later that night, Razz, Chris, and a few other Deep Water Cay managers and I were sitting in a high-end restaurant (aka fancy pizza joint) in Palm Beach. We were enjoying several very expensive pizzas and washing them down with Abita Brewing Company's Andygator and the occasional Purple Haze. Actually, it was a fifty/fifty mix of Andygator and Purple Haze. It's the ultimate beer cocktail. I can only point you in the right direction and get out of your way; the rest is up to you, but if you love beer, it's something you should try.

It was getting late, and I was ready to hit the sack. I can only assume that the half a dozen slices of pizza and the steady flow of cocktails didn't help the situation either. Chris and I had been up since early morning. We were about to stand up and take our leave when someone at the table suggested that we needed to make a video for the new website I was building for Deep Water Cay. It was almost finished, but Paul hadn't approved it yet. Paul Vahldiek is the owner of Deep Water Cay, one of the most iconic bonefish lodges in the Atlantic outside of maybe Casa Blanca on the Yucatán Peninsula. The Bahamas lie just north of the Lesser Antilles and southeast of Palm Beach. Deep Water Cay lies several miles southeast of Grand Bahama Island. For some reason, people want to keep lumping the Bahamas into the Caribbean. That's like saying the Gulf of Mexico is actually the Atlantic Ocean, and relatively speaking it is, but then again, it's not, it's the Gulf of Mexico. Semantics do matter!

Paul was part of a group of investors that also owned various other high-end ranches and lodges in Colorado. My other company, Integrated Digital Publishing, had handled the marketing contract for all three properties for the last several years. It was an exciting idea, and I knew better than anyone that there was plenty of money left in the budget. Even though I'm not sure Deep Water Cay had what you would call a real budget. It was more like a slush fund to which just about everyone seemed to have access. Regardless of the money in the "budget," we still needed to get Paul's approval. Before we ran it by Paul, I wanted to put a proposal together that included dates, video, editing, and custom soundtrack all within a reasonable budget. Personally, I didn't consider the cost that important. Of course, I wasn't privy to what went on behind the iron curtain. Several years earlier, Paul went all-in on a similar project for the High Lonesome Ranch and the K-T Ranch. I didn't see any reason why he wouldn't do the same this time around. Paul was easy to deal with; it was all the little sycophants that surrounded him that always caused problems. They continually felt the need to chime in regardless of whether they knew what they were talking about. This was different. It wasn't my idea; I was just the one creating the video. I was more than happy to let the other minions do the heavy lifting!

I had been working with the same production company for the last several years. They were relatively expensive but were very good at what they did. Everything was done in-house; nothing was canned. Creating a quality video with sound can be complicated, and the number of people needed to pull it off grows exponentially with each additional camera. The video's quality depended on the number of chase boats, not to mention the fisherman's boat. That meant we needed a minimum of four guides, four flats boats, and room and board for the camera crews, the director, Chris Pipes, and me for a week. Then there was the expense of the flights down and back and all the additional baggage.

To make things worse, we had to get permits from the Bahamian government to bring all the gear into the Bahamas. We had to pay additional taxes based on the cost of the cameras and the rest of the equipment. To clear customs, the majority of the gear had to arrive early. It was beginning to get a little overwhelming! Then someone mentioned something about renting a helicopter (I kept thinking the US Navy sounded cheaper). Paul gave us the thumbs-up. I just wish he had informed the manager at Deep Water Cay we were coming and what we intended to do when we got there.

Three weeks later, we all started arriving via different airlines at different times throughout the day. We needed to pick up the gear at the customs building, then find transportation to the city docks, where someone from Deep Water Cay was supposed to pick us up and take us over to the island. Of course, when we got to the docks no one was there. Chris got on the phone and called the lodge and managed to get someone to pick us up. When they finally arrived, they were in complete horror. They had no idea this many people and this much gear was involved in making a simple video—and they hadn't even met Isaias yet. Isaias is one of my closest friends and a world-class photographer from Patagonia, who was due to arrive later that day.

Evidently, Paul forgot to tell them anything about the production crew and the gear. Fortunately for us, Paul put us up in his private home on the beach. Unfortunately for us, the lodge was almost full, which meant the majority of the boats needed to make the video had to be set aside for the paying customers. Even worse, some of Paul's minions and their families were there, and they had no idea who or why we were there. They seemed a little taken aback when they finally learned how much it would cost them to watch us sit around and play pool and spend copious amounts of time at the tiki bar, drowning our sorrow at their expense.

The manager and his wife were some of the nicest people on the planet, but they had no idea what to do. No one seemed brave enough to call Paul and complain. Knowing Paul, he probably would have jumped in his private jet and been down there before sunset. This was a clusterf*** in the making. It could only get worse and, somehow we still needed to make the film. So, we did what most fishermen the world over would have done: That evening we pigged out on fresh conch and red snapper and finished the night on the beach drinking rumrunners and howling at the moon. Little did we know at the time, but there was an angry lady named Sandy bearing down on the Bahamas.

If You See a Hurricane, Hooper, Swallow!

FISHERMEN COME IN SO MANY FLAVORS IT'S HARD TO PIN ONE DOWN. There is no such thing as the average fisherman, and given a dangerous situation, you never know how one will respond. Some fishermen live their life with one foot in the grave, while others stand in the middle of a cow pasture in the midst of a raging thunderstorm and dare Zeus to drive a lightning bolt through their chest. Others take life one day at a time and move on. There is no right or wrong. It's just the nature of the beast. I've noticed that, to some extent, one fisherman can be happy just sitting on the bank of the Saint Johns River with a cane pole catching a stringer full of redbreast, while another fisherman can't be happy unless he is pitching flies to a thirty-pound permit somewhere in the Yucatán. Fishermen are diverse creatures, if nothing else.

Mention the word hurricane and the response depends typically on where you grew up and your predisposition to extreme weather. Fortunately, or unfortunately, depending on your proclivity, large waves can drive your inner demons and radically change the way you perceive the world. I grew up in South Florida, and when the hurricane flags started to stand on end, my friends and I started waxing down our surfboards. Of course, we were young and dumb and full of piss and vinegar, but we were fearless, if nothing else.

When the news started floating around the lodge about Hurricane Sandy, most of the fishermen began packing, and within the next few days, the lodge was almost empty. However, to my disbelief, there were still new customers arriving, and one customer who had been there for the last month and had no intention of leaving. I promised I would never write about him or use any photographs with him in them, but his last name was Hemingway. There might have been a few generations between him and Papa. Most of the Hemingway family has done their best to put some distance between themselves and their famous father, but not this one; he did his best to walk in Papa's shoes. I could write a book about the late-night conversations we had at the bar. Of course, we closed the bar down every night, until finally the bartender capitulated and gave us the keys. It was something I paid dearly for the next several mornings. I guess some things never change. I am still the dumb kid full of piss and vinegar, just a little older.

The next morning, I got a phone call from Paul. Somewhere in the dead of night, he decided that a large part of the video should be about permit fishing. I could only assume that he knew how difficult it was to catch a permit on a fly. Who knows, maybe one of Paul's little minions suggested it! But we had more important things to worry about at the moment—besides the Category 3 hurricane about to come screaming through the Lesser Antilles hell-bent for leather. We needed four flats boats and quickly. Then I tried my best to change Paul's mind. I wasn't opposed to chasing permit, but to go out and catch one on demand seemed a little ridiculous given the time constraints and a hurricane breathing down our neck. After I stopped Chris from laughing, we sat down with the film crew and began to sketch out a plan. Soon it just started to come together. An idea here and a suggestion there; it's amazing how things always seem to make sense sitting around the breakfast table over coffee (assuming you're not suffering from a hangover from the previous night).

Paul finally persuaded the manager to give us the four boats. I knew he was under extreme duress and only knuckled under for fear of losing his job. To provide us with the new Hells Bay flats boats, he had to give paying customers some of the older boats. They're just wasn't any way around it.

Some very productive permit flats stretched out southeast of Deep Water Cay. In fact, they're some of the best flats I have ever fished. But to get to them, you had to run across a lot of open water and then back again. Most of the time, guests wake up and take a leisurely shower, blow-dry their hair, and eventually meet the other guests for breakfast in the main dining room. Then they casually carry their gear down to the boats and meet their guide for the day. If they're lucky, they're on the water and running by eight-thirty. We did our best to convince the guides to have our boats loaded and ready to run at dawn.

The next morning, we were standing at the end of the dock waiting for the guides to show up. I guess it was a little too much to expect from the Bahamian guides, to get up and moving before sunrise. We eventually gave up and went back inside for more coffee, and later that morning, we had breakfast with the other guests. The guides finally showed up a few minutes before eight and started loading the boats. I was upset, but I didn't say anything. No one wanted to get off to a bad start. Thankfully, it was a beautiful day. There wasn't a cloud in the sky, and the ocean was as flat as glass. It seemed a little eerie at the time, the proverbial calm before the storm. The hurricane was seven or eight days out. We still had plenty of time to do what we came here to do and get the hell out before the storm arrived. We were fighting the tides as much as anything. We had already lost the first two hours of the early flood, and we still had a long run ahead of us. The longer we waited, the poorer our chances of seeing any permit up on the flats, much less convincing one to take a fly. About this time, I would have given almost anything for a livewell full of pass crabs.

It took awhile to load all the gear into the right boats. We still needed to have an in-depth conversation with the four guides to make sure we were all on the same page. We had no idea if they even understood what we were doing. As far as I knew, they likely thought we were going fishing. Chris and I were in the lead skiff, and the other three skiffs would follow; once someone spotted a permit, the guides would turn the controls of the boat over to the cameramen. That didn't go over very well either!

Adding to the confusion, this was the first fly-fishing video the production crew had ever made. For the most part, the crew couldn't tell the difference between a permit and a tarpon (and I'm being generous here). Chris and I stared at each other for several seconds without saying a word. Honestly, we had no idea what was going to happen. Isaias jumped in the boat with Chris and me, with what looked like several hundred pounds of camera gear. The Three Stooges ride again! I sighed as we pushed away from the docks. By this time, there were twenty or so guests and employees standing on the docks watching us. Some of them were wishing us luck, and others reminded me of the people standing on the pier waving goodbye to the *Titanic*. We could only be so lucky! Then again, it was just another adventure, and it had to start somewhere. Isaias turned and reminded me of the tagline for Sweet Waters Adventure, "Where Life is an Adventure Not a Guided Tour."

What idiot said that? Chris just chuckled.

Admiral, There Be Permit Here

As we idled out of the estuary, we spooked school after school of bonefish delicately working their way in and out of the mangrove roots—a dimple here, a dimple there; it was a beautiful sight! Tails gleamed in the sun, and puffs of mud everywhere indicated feeding fish. There were dozens of wading birds picking their way through the mangrove shoots, snatching a glass minnow here and there. Now and again the occasional ray blew off the flats, flushed by the methodic rumble of the big outboards. It was a world taken directly from a Chet Reneson painting, a world that seemed to belong to him, a world only he could capture. I kept taking mental snapshots of alternative landscapes that caught my eye, and out-of-the-way little fisheries in case things got too bad on the open ocean.

A few minutes later we were off and running. Even in twenty feet of water, you could count the individual leaves of turtle grass. Bottlenose dolphins playfully escorted us out to sea. We ran across massive schools of baitfish that seemed to be cruising along as if they didn't have a care in the world. Life began to slow down and take on a more primordial pace that restores us to our original designation as a part of nature, not its adversary. It was simple, right? All we had to do was show up, make a great cast, hook a big permit, and land it, *and* get it all on film and call it a take. Of course, no one in the boat gave us much of a chance, and why should they? It's a permit for Christ's sake. Anyone with half a brain would have stayed in bed and called in sick. I had been fishing for permit for the last twenty-five years, and the one thing it's never been was easy. It usually required eight to ten hours a day staring into the abyss, hoping, then wishing, then praying to a select assortment of deities to lend a helping hand. More often than not, the gods treated me like a dog. Somewhere, somehow, I must have done something in a previous life to offend them, and they appear to never have forgotten it.

After a forty- or forty-five-minute boat ride, we backed off the throttle, came off plane almost simultaneously, and idled into the back door of a vast basin. The tide was low enough yet that some of the sandbars were still exposed. The guides immediately stood up and started pointing to something. I picked up a pair of binoculars lying on the center console and started scanning the water for any signs of permit. Then out of nowhere, another guide started screaming something about three different schools of fish.

Mike (aka cell phone Mike) shut the engine down, climbed up on the poling platform, and started poling his way down the left side of one of the massive flats. The last thing Mike wanted to do was spook the fish. After climbing up on the casting platform, I started stripping sixty or seventy feet of fly line off the reel. Then I started making a few false casts to begin stacking the fly line from bottom to top, so the line didn't get tangled when I finally needed to make a cast. The water was transparent. I didn't think we could ever get close enough to make a good cast without spooking the permit. By this time, the camera boats had started positioning themselves so they could cover almost any angle. Then out of nowhere, twenty feet directly in front of the skiff, we spotted a giant mud and two large tails trying to dig out a crab or maybe a fresh lobster for breakfast.

The permit was utterly oblivious to the boat. I made one false cast and dropped a weighted Merkin right on top of their heads. I let it sink to the bottom and gave it one small twitch, and in the immortal word of Emeril Lagasse, "Bam!" I stripped and set the fly several times, and we were off to the races! It was just that easy. For the moment, all I could do was stand there and listen to the Tibor play that funky music. Unfortunately, it had happened so fast the cameramen had missed both the cast and the hookup. By the time they managed to get the cameras rolling, the permit was headed southeast somewhere in South Andros's direction. Like all big permit, it didn't have any intention of slugging it out in shallow water. If it managed to drop off the edge of the reef, more than likely the fish would cut me off on all the coral and sea fans that traditionally line the drop-offs. I did my best to talk Mike into dropping the engine so I could get some line back on the reel and hopefully keep the fish on the fly line. By this time the permit was several hundred yards into my backing, which meant I had very little control of the situation.

After I pleaded for what seemed like hours, Mike finally started the engine. It had to be done, but this is where it got a bit tricky. Mike could only go so fast without introducing slack line into the fight. I had to reel like a screaming banshee to keep the line tight. In the midst of all the mayhem, the strangest thing happened. The permit turned and bolted back into the basin. I tried my best to get as much line back on the reel as possible. We were now headed back in the same direction we came from. I have to admit that was the last thing I expected, and by the time Mike got the boat turned around, there was so much slack line lying on the water, I thought the fish was gone for sure. I reeled like a madman possessed by some poor soul that didn't have a silver obol to pay Charon to ferry him across to the River Styx. Mike put the skiff in reverse in hopes of getting the slack line back, employing virtually the same method used to stop a runaway locomotive!

I backed off on the drag as much as possible. When we reached the critical point where all the slack was gone, I knew things were not going to end well, so I started throwing as much slack line as I could back into the water until the line came tight and Mike took the engine out of reverse. When we reached the point of contact, the permit felt the tension on the line, and it took off again, headed to the far end of the basin. I tightened the drag, at least to the point where I felt comfortable. Slowly but surely, I started to gain some line back. It was only a few inches at a time, but it was line nonetheless. We didn't necessarily win the first round, but for all practical purposes, we had survived it! At least at this point, I was almost back on the fly line.

Twenty or thirty minutes later, I could sense the permit was getting tired. Why shouldn't the fish be getting tired? Hell, I was getting tired! I think the cameramen never dreamed it would take this long to fight and land a permit. Then again, I don't think they had any idea how big a large permit could be. To be honest, though, it wasn't what you might call a giant permit. It was probably somewhere around twenty-two, maybe twenty-three pounds. I have no idea what really constitutes a big permit. I guess you know one when you see it.

Ten, maybe fifteen minutes later, the fish finally started circling the skiff. Normally that's a good sign, meaning the fight is almost over. Of course, that's when things usually start to fall apart. A few minutes later, the fish was almost at arm's length, still too strong to manhandle, but almost close enough to grab his tail. I was doing everything in my power to prevent the permit from making one last run. In retrospect, I should have let the fish run again. The three camera boats had circled the skiff. Then the unthinkable happened. A ten- or twelve-inch barracuda came screaming out from under the skiff and cut me off at the knot. Seconds later, I was standing there looking at my fly line waving in the wind. There is absolutely no way I could have anticipated something like this would happen, but I have to admit that I was partially to blame.

I hate store-bought leaders. The butt section on a knotless tapered leader is never heavy enough to turn over the heavy flies we use in salt-water. That's why I have always taken the time to make my own leaders. I also detest the ubiquitous loop-to-loop connections that come with the new fly lines. The first thing I do with a new fly line is cut the damn loop off, and then I nail-knot a three-foot piece of fifty-pound test monofilament to the fly line and build my leader from there. Unfortunately, one of the knots was skimming across the surface of the water creating a chain of air bubbles behind it. The little barracuda couldn't resist the knot. It's the same thing that happens when you're standing on a pier and casting crocks at mackerel. I can't tell you how many spoons I've lost to mackerel over the years because the fish went after the knot instead of the spoon. I have said it many times: It's the price we pay to play the game! And in the end, it is just a game.

Sitting on the casting deck, looking back at Mike and Chris, I could only shrug my shoulders and move on. I was rehashing in my head all the things that went right and all the things we did wrong. Win or lose, every permit provides an opportunity for a moment of quiet introspection. The last thing I was going to do was beat myself up over a lost fish. Chris handed me a beer, and as I was opened it, I heard the camera crew and a couple of the guides whooping and hollering in the background. Several hundred yards down the flat, they were chasing the permit around the shallow water as if they really thought they could grab the fish by the tail. The fish was tired, but the odds of catching the permit by the tail were ten million to one at best. We stood a better chance of getting a date with Léa Seydoux. The upside, if you could really consider it an upside, was that one of the cameramen was getting all of this on film. It was getting a little embarrassing. I tied up a new leader, tied on another Merkin, and climbed back up on the casting platform. Mike hustled onto the poling platform and did his best to push us off the sandbar. The day was still young, and the tide was still rising, and we had a permit to catch!

We needed to find the other permit, the ones the guides spotted when we first poled into the basin. Permit fishing is not for the faint-hearted. The results are generally based on the amount of time you spend on the water and, maybe more importantly, where that water is. We were poling down some of the best permit flats on the planet, yet I didn't have any higher expectations than when we first arrived. We poled our way east for the next several hours, and a half hour before the tide was due to change, we spotted two massive tails. They were slowly cruising along the drop-off of a small grass flat that eventually turned into a long sandbar. It was one of the few times I have ever had the opportunity to see a massive permit broadside this close. It looked like they were headed for the open ocean but didn't seem to be in any hurry to get there. We froze. I was terrified even to take a breath. At any moment, I expected them to bolt like a rocket sled on wheels, or at the very least, fade away into the landscape.

Now came the multimillion-dollar question. The permit were swimming right to left. The fish weren't feeding, so there was no mud in the water. There was nothing to take their mind off what was about to happen, yet you still have to make the cast. So where do you put the fly? Volumes have been written on this very topic, but in the end, it comes down to taking your best shot and hoping for a little luck.

Mike just started laughing. He knew exactly what I was going through, so much so he refused to chime in. The experts will tell you to drop the fly on their heads, but that's a one in a million shot in water this clear, especially when they're not actively feeding. Then again, I could only assume that the two behemoths were on the flats looking for food and not a morning constitutional. I was driving myself mad with indecision until I finally made a long, lazy cast about thirty feet in front of the fish, well up on the sandbar. I admit, it was the coward's way out.

When the fly hit the water, the two fish stopped on a dime. Now what the hell do you do? The second most discussed question about permit fishing is: to twitch or not to twitch. Do I tease or let the fly lie? The next thing I knew, the fish had lost interest and were working their way up the sandbar. They were coming shallow a few inches at a time. Unfortunately, that put them on a collision course with my fly line. I dropped the rod tip and tried to lay my fly line on the bottom. It was almost impossible—I was using a floating line. Still, I stripped the line hard, hoping that the heavy Merkin would throw up some sand and draw their attention. Instead, the two fish exploded across the flat, and seconds later, we watched them make a beeline for the open ocean and disappear. With the tide dropping fast, we decided it was time to chase some bonefish. It was time to rip some lips and purge the frustration out of my system. At least we knew there were fish here. The tide would be an hour later tomorrow, and we planned on getting an earlier start, if possible.

Stupid Is as Stupid Does

After a hot shower and a cold beer, I walked back down to the docks to talk to Mike before he left for the day. I wanted to make sure we had an ironclad plan for the next morning. We wanted to be on the water and heading east at daybreak. No more ifs, ands, or buts about it this time. We didn't want to repeat the same snafu we experienced this morning. I was sitting on a bench watching Mike clean the skiff. I was tossing out a few ideas here and there when he looked up and said, "I don't think we are fishing together tomorrow."

When I inquired why, he just shrugged his shoulders and told me, "Go talk to the manager; I don't make the schedule."

Virtually all companies are the same. They're layered from bottom to top with everything from flunkies to middle managers to the general manager, CEOs, and CFOs. Sprinkled in this eclectic menagerie of wannabes, you have the various investors. Some participate if given a chance; others hide in the shadows like vampires. They come out at night and suck the life out of an organization. The problem is that regardless of who they are or what their job title might be, they sit around and think of ways to screw each other, or in this case, me! They smile to your face, and when you turn and walk away, they bury a rusty fillet knife in your back. They can't help themselves; it's who they are. They hate you because you're different and don't play by the same rules, and as hard as they try, they have little if any influence on your life, and it drives them absolutely mad!

One of the minority owners took it upon himself to invite some of his friends and family down to Deep Water Cay for the next three days. He needed all the boats that were not being used by paying customers for his friends and business associates. I think if Paul had known about it, he probably would have grabbed him by the seat of his pants and pitched his sorry ass off the dock. Come to find out later, his so-called business associates didn't have anything to do with Deep Water Cay. Of course, it wasn't me that was getting screwed. It was Paul. I did my best not to rock the boat. We needed a day off to film the lodge and all the amenities anyway. Meanwhile, Chris did his best to solve our ongoing issues. Chris is a diplomat at heart, and knowing his proclivity to get his way, he was the perfect person to deal with all of Paul's little sycophants. The only option I had at the time was to call Paul again and hope for the best, but at the same time, the last thing I wanted to do was alienate Paul's minions. The best-laid plans of mice and men always seem to fail in ways that you could never anticipate. In the end, you work with what you have and make the best of the situation.

Chris made an extensive list of things we needed to shoot and another list that could have been considered a wish list of sorts. If we had to, we could spend the next two days shooting the lodge, tiki bar, and the beaches, and when the tide was right, we could wade the beachside flats and chase bonefish. Still, if we wanted another opportunity at catching a permit, we needed boats and guides, and more importantly, we needed to be on the outside flats where the fish were.

There comes a time when you need to be honest with yourself. I was sitting at the tiki bar waiting for dinner, having a Slow Comfort Screw Up Against the Wall, a cocktail I discovered last year in Belize. A part of me would have moved mountains to get back on the permit flats we were fishing this morning. I knew the video was going to be great regardless of whether or not I caught a big permit, and in the grand scope of things, it was only a small part of the project. In fact, for all practical purposes, other than getting what would eventually amount to ten or fifteen seconds of film, we didn't need a permit. Yet here I was, scheming of ways to get back on the water tomorrow. I had to keep reminding myself the video was supposed to be about Deep Water Cay, and not about Jim Stenson catching a thirty-pound permit.

I have always prided myself on being a reasonable and often rational person who loves his wife and family and would do anything for them. But here I sit, considering getting a second and maybe a third mortgage and outfitting a mother ship with several flats boats and spending the remaining days of my life chasing permit. The flats were so close I could taste them. I could feel the pull of the tides. I was obsessed with permit, even mesmerized to the point of stealing one of the Hells Bay skiffs in the morning and going it alone. If caught, I could easily plead temporary insanity!

Lost in my reverie, I didn't realize that everyone else was having dinner. When I finally made my way to the dining room, a couple of the film crew just started laughing. They had been calling me for dinner for the last twenty minutes until they finally gave up. Maybe it's time to stay away from any cocktail with that long a name.

The next morning, we watched a half dozen paying customers and four or five freeloaders put to sea. The moron that arranged this little escapade stood a few feet from me, smiling and waving at his friends and family. He turned and said something snarky and started to walk away. I couldn't help myself. I said, "I hope you're happy. You just cost Paul in the neighborhood of twenty thousand dollars for the day, asswipe."

Maybe "asswipe" was a little over the top, but I was a bit upset. As the moron was walking away, I could not help but shout, "If it were my lodge, I would feed your sorry ass to the sharks."

It's not something you might read in *How to Win Friends and Influence Enemies*. Then again, he obviously knew where I stood.

At times like this, discretion may be the better part of valor, but it's not in my nature to be that discreet. Unfortunately, it rarely pays dividends, and like Hemingway, I can be an ass sometimes. The film crew didn't need me; they had their shot list for the day. So I grabbed my fly rod and a small box of bonefish flies and proceeded to fish the flats on the front side of the island. I needed to cool off, and the best way to calm down was to get away from people. Deep Water Cay is a long island, and the ocean-side flats are substantial and seem to run on forever. If I wanted to, I could spend the day sight-fishing for whatever came along and never fish the same flat twice.

I had barely made my way to the water when I head Isaias walk up behind me sporting a backpack and a fanny pack filled with fly boxes. The backpack was full of sandwiches and a few beers. Isaias is one of the few people on the planet that I am always happy to see. I think he knew deep down inside that I was not nearly as upset as I was pretending to be. Over the last fifteen years, Isaias has been one of my closest friends and confidants. I met him and his family in Argentina sixteen years ago. His father, Georg Miciu Nicolaevici, is one of the leading impressionist painters of our time, and through the years, he has been incredibly kind and generous to a fault when it comes to my wife and myself. He painted the cover of my wife's first book, *Winds of Change*, and several months ago, he painted the cover of my first book, titled *Where the Sweet Meet the Brine*.

I handed the fly rod to Isaias and told him, "I will play guide today; just concentrate on the bonefish."

I knew this was going to be a treat for Isaias. He is one of the best outdoor photographers in the world, but is in such high demand these days, we hardly ever get the opportunity to spend some quality time on the water together. He loves to fly fish, but fortunately or unfortunately, depending on how you look at it, he rarely gets the opportunity to put the camera down and pick up a fly rod.

I usually hate to guide, especially people I don't know very well. Good relationships take years, if not decades, to develop. Generally, if I find myself guiding someone, it's because I've known them for a long time and I cherish their friendship. It's not guiding in the traditional sense. It's more like spending some quality time on the water fishing with a close friend.

We were wading east across a rocky flat covered with sea fans and grooved brain coral and the occasional elkhorn coral interspersed among the grass flats. The flats were thick with silversides, queen angelfish, sergeant majors in all flavors, and a multitude of other tropical fish I couldn't recognize at the time. There were hordes of various kinds of parrotfish nibbling away at the coral and empty conch shells scattered along the flats like litter.

It belonged to a world I hadn't visited in a long time. At the time, I seriously thought about trading in my fly rod for a mask and a pair of fins. A few stingrays flushed as we made our way down the flat. In the distance, we saw several schools of bonefish zigzagging across the flats as the tide began to flood. We could see giant cumulus clouds starting to form on the horizon. They had the traditional deep purples, blacks, and pink undertones, which foreshadowed the onset of ominous weather. It reminded me of growing up on Anglings pier, watching the late-afternoon thunderstorms that came rolling in across the Everglades. I took a deep breath, and after several minutes, the stress and aggravation of the morning slowly dissipated. I just smiled!

For someone who grew up in Argentina, Isaias seemed to be at home in the salt. After twenty minutes on the flats, I would have sworn he grew up somewhere in the tropics chasing bonefish. He looked at ease, navigating his way in and out of the minefield along the flat, especially for someone who I knew had spent his life floating the famous rivers of Patagonia and Tierra del Fuego. In fact, he never stopped telling me stories about the high-altitude streams in the Andes and the deep lakes above tree line where his brothers and sisters spent their childhood chasing giant rainbows and brook trout. When I first met Isaias, it didn't take me long to realize that he was much more than just a photographer; he's an artist posing as a photographer. Georg trained Isaias to be an artist when he was young, fully expecting him to carry on in his footsteps, but somewhere along the line, he picked up a camera, and the rest, as they say, is history.

Isaias and I had a choice. We could either stand still and hope the fish moved our way or make our way east in hopes of finding some fish closer to shore. Wading for bonefish and permit is the ultimate sport, and at the same time, it can be one of the most frustrating things you can do with a fly rod. You're always at a disadvantage because you're so low to the water. On the other hand, it's incredible how close you can get to the fish if you're stealthy enough. It's the old game of cat and mouse, and it can go on for what seems like hours. The last thing you want to do is push the situation, make a bad cast, and spook the fish. You're almost on your knees—hell, sometimes you are on your knees—trying to get as low to the water as possible. You're creeping along a few inches at a time. You're continually tripping and stumbling over the coral and rocks because you don't want to lose sight of the bonefish. If you are lucky, the fish are moving in your direction, and all you have to do is hunker down and wait. I have chased bonefish around a flat for hours, trying to get into position to make a good cast, before finally spooking the school and watching them blast off in all directions.

I have waited for what seemed like days to get in a perfect position to make a cast, only to have a pelican buzz the school like a fighter jet and spook it to kingdom come and back. And the beat goes on. Then there are the times when you do everything right, and the gods finally step in and decide you have had enough and reward you with a huge bonefish. In the end, you have to go with your intuition and take your best shot. At some point, you have to come to terms with the realization that you're chasing a fish with a brain the size of a pencil eraser, but with the honed instincts of a fighter pilot.

Wading for permit usually requires a boat and the expert eyes of a guide. It helps to have a skiff to move around the various flats. Once you spot a few fish, you can then get out and stalk the permit on foot. That allows the guide to stand on the poling platform and get a better view of the situation, then bark out the distance and direction. It's like having an eye in the sky! Depending on where you're fishing, odds are there will be exponentially more bonefish than permit. For the most part, permit tend to like deeper flats, where wading can be difficult at best. Bonefish tend to like shallow flats, even though nothing is written in stone. I am speaking in generalities here, and I know there are thousands of variations on the theme.

It's always been easier to catch permit in deeper water on live baits. In the late 1960s and early 1970s, we used to chase bonefish and the occasional permit on the ocean-side flats of the Florida Keys—especially before the mass exodus of people from the Northeast and the Midwest moved south and developed the upper keys. Upper Card Sound Road was always a great place to start. The ocean-side flats on Upper and Lower Matecumbe Key were consistently productive and extremely popular with fly fishermen. And believe it or not, you could find the occasional permit there on the right tide. Of course, finding one and catching one are two completely different things. As far as Isaias and me running into a permit on the ocean-side flats of Deep Water Cay, it was entirely within the realm of possibility. Then again, I might trip over a piece of pottery and accidentally discover the lost city of Atlantis. One never knows about such things!

Of course, I'm not saying it couldn't happen. But when you spend six or seven thousand dollars a week to fish Deep Water Cay, you usually don't spend much time wading the flats that surround the lodge. You jump into a sixty-thousand-dollar flats boat with a giant Yamaha and blast off to some distant destination that, for whatever reason, is supposed to be better than the one we were now wading. Considering how little pressure the ocean-side flats actually get, we probably had a better than even chance to at least see a few permit. At this point in my life, very few things shock me anymore, but I am always optimistic. Once the number and size of the fish you catch is no longer the reason you do this, the game's parameters change, and you find you tend to be a much happier fisherman. That being said, I can't think of a better way of spending the day than chasing, hooking, and landing a thirty-pound permit in front of the lodge. It almost seems poetic. I could only hope Isaias had a camera in his pack somewhere.

We didn't catch a permit that day, but we did land a half dozen bonefish. Nothing to write home about, but we had a blast nonetheless. By the end of the day, we had covered several miles of shoreline. Like most tourists, we spent almost as much time exploring as we did fishing. When we finally returned to the lodge, the film crew had already showered and made their way to the tiki bar. Everyone seemed in good spirits. They kept asking me about the next day and what was going to happen. Isaias and I climbed into the golf cart and headed back to the house to clean up for dinner. Suddenly, I impulsively pulled off the road at the lodge office. Isaias tried to prevent me from going in, but I ignored him and marched into the office to see what was going on. Isaias is a pacifist at heart. On the other hand, I tend to take the "death from above" approach to problem-solving. Life is too short to compromise.

The bullshit had to end now. Before I opened my mouth, I looked at the board to see what the schedule looked like for the next day. Apparently, some of the moron's friends were getting a little nervous about the hurricane. Another day of fishing seemed less important than getting stranded on Deep Water Cay during a storm. They were already on their way back to the airport with the imbecile in tow. We had our boats back, at least for the next few days. The powers that be, however, had decided to start battening down the hatches. They wanted to get the boats back in the barn as soon as possible. Grand Bahama was only a mile or so away, but you had to cross open water to get there. Looking out the window, I didn't see a cloud in the sky, and other than the wake of an occasional commercial fishing boat, the ocean looked like a sheet of glass.

Like most nights, we enjoyed a hearty dinner that seemed to always start with fresh conch fritters, followed by a healthy salad of sorts sprinkled with fresh shrimp or lobster and a homemade dressing of the chef's liking. The main course always consisted of fresh seafood of some type, most likely caught that day. Even the pasta dishes contained fresh seafood. My favorite was the grilled hog snapper stuffed with shrimp, lobster, and scallops in a hearty champagne sauce made using heavy cream and various hard cheeses like Parmigiano-Reggiano or maybe some aged Asiago. The desserts were always over the top, though by the time you finished dinner and downed several cocktails, regardless of how good the desserts looked, it didn't seem possible to eat them, yet some of the younger kids devoured them. The dining room was gorgeous! The walls were covered with dozens of photos of famous fishermen who once called Deep Water Cay their homeport. The place was and still is legendary. Fishermen like A. J. McClane, Lefty Kreh, Joe Brooks, Stu Apt, Ted Williams, and many others chased bonefish and permit on the same flats we were fishing. We were fishing in the footsteps of legends.

Those of us who had the stomach, and I would like to say the stamina, to stagger over to the tiki bar were rewarded or punished, depending on your perspective, with some of the wildest, if not the most lethal, concoctions known to man. Of course, no one died that night, but it's safe to say it took weeks for some of the film crew to recover. Kids! We lined up at the ring game and played for drinks for hours. Eventually some of the film crew crawled over to the pool and crashed on several of the beach recliners for the night.

Later that night, I was sound asleep when I heard a loud noise on the porch. Most of us were sleeping with the curtains pulled back and the windows wide open. For some reason, it was relatively cool that night, and the fresh ocean air was very much appreciated after the rather late night at the tiki bar. I didn't want to get up. At first, I just assumed it was one of the boys who fell asleep by the pool and finally staggered home and tripped over something on the porch. Then I heard it again, so I crawled out of bed and gingerly walked, maybe crawled, over to the window to see what all the commotion was about. From what I could tell, the wind had blown several beach chairs off the porch. Then I noticed the surf. It wasn't exactly roaring, but it seemed a little angry. I crawled back into bed and decided I wouldn't worry about it until tomorrow morning, and then it dawned on me that we had to meet the guides at sunup.

A few hours later, I crawled into the shower, dressed, and slowly made my way to the main lodge in the hopes of finding some fresh coffee. Fortunately, the kitchen staff was in early and in the process of making coffee, a wonderful blend of hazelnut and cinnamon. You could smell it as far away as the tiki bar, the site of last night's debauchery. I took my coffee and walked down to the beach to see what the water looked like. The wind was out of the southeast at maybe ten to fifteen miles an hour. The water was choppy, but from what I could see, it didn't look dirty. It was still early, but in the distance, I could see huge thunderstorms making their way through the islands. The hurricane was still five or six days out. I doubt the storms were even related to the hurricane. Regardless of the reason, though, it was going to be a wet day.

It was obvious no one was in any hurry to push off that morning. The guides were a little hesitant to make the long run needed to reach the leeward side of Grand Bahama Island. It hardly seemed worth the trouble, but we wanted to get out of the wind and play with a few innocent bonefish. It wasn't necessarily the trip over that they were worried about, but the trip back. I was getting a little frustrated, but I didn't want to make them do anything they didn't want to do in the first place. The film crew just wanted to crawl back into bed and call it a day. I eventually lost patience and blurted out, "Give me the keys to the skiff and get the hell out of my way!"

I kept mumbling something like: "For Christ's sake, this is the tropics and the damn wind is supposed to blow! You picked the damnedest profession for someone that's scared of a little wind and rain. Get a life, or better yet get a new job. Even better, get a new girlfriend; this one is going to cost you your job sooner than later."

I have always been amazed at the lengths some people will go to make you believe they only have your best interest in mind, when they actually couldn't care less. The truth is Mike probably wanted to spend the day with his girlfriend. We call him "cell phone Mike" because every time you turn around, he's on his cell phone talking to his girlfriend. How he has the time to spot any fish, I will never know!

I finally gave in and let the guides do whatever they wanted. By the time we made it back to the house, you could barely see ten feet in front of you. The winds were beginning to resemble heavy squalls, and the massive sheets of rain fell almost horizontal. We were soaked by the time we made it to the front porch. I suggested to the film crew that they should start loading their gear. That way, if the storm subsided overnight, we might be able to get a few more hours of fishing in before we had to leave. I didn't want to bring it up, but if the storms increased in strength overnight, we might get stuck here for a few extra days. Either that or we'd have to call the mainland for a larger boat to pick us up.

Our flight was scheduled to leave Grand Bahama in the late afternoon, but the film crew would have to go through customs and drop their gear off first, before they boarded the flight. I never quite figured that one out. I had no idea why the camera equipment couldn't go back on the same flight we were on. I kept telling them, "Make sure you have all the files on your carry-on hard drive. Just in case something happens to your camera gear."

Of course, they looked at me like I was stupid, as if it was something they hadn't already considered. It was getting a little testy; I didn't know if they were in a hurry to leave or if it was the hangovers talking. I spent the next few hours packing, but I did leave one rod out in case we got the opportunity to get back on the water.

The boys had shot a tremendous amount of film, but for some reason I felt cheated. I was still thinking about the permit I lost. I rarely remember all the details of the permit I've caught. On the other hand, I remember every detail of the fish I've lost. Like I mentioned earlier, when it comes to permit, the gods tend to treat me like a dog. I rarely catch a break! Maybe it's supposed to be that way. Who knows? That would explain the lack of fishermen willing to put up with the aggravation and the necessary expense required to chase permit.

I have to admit, the day pretty much sucked! The wind kept blowing and the rain never seemed to let up. It made getting down to the lodge problematic at best, even wearing quality rain gear. At some point, I gave up. A little rain never hurt anyone, and like I told Mike, it's supposed to rain in the tropics. I spent the day playing pool while some of the other guys played cards, and when we got bored, we put on our rain gear and walked out to the docks and just stared into the water, as if it was going to help in some way or the other!

That night at dinner, our group appeared a little melancholy at times. The trip was coming to an end. Everyone realized that they were headed home in the morning, back to the real world with real problems with real-world consequences. Sure, everyone was looking forward to getting back to their families. In some ways, they had had the opportunity to live the kind of life I lived 250 days a year, give or take a few weeks. In three weeks I would be in western Alaska floating the Kanektok River for ten days, chasing double-digit rainbows, and they would be back at work, dealing with the daily grind of owning a successful tech company. Both jobs require a certain amount of time and effort, not to mention stress. On the other hand, they didn't have to deal with the possibility of a five- or six-hundred-pound grizzly chewing their ass off either.

We turned in early that night. I was having a difficult time sleeping. Maybe I was a little stressed, who knows? Other than the occasional gust, the winds seem to have quieted down. The torrential rains we had experienced throughout the day had all but stopped. I broke down my fly rod and packed it into my rod case and stacked my gear by the door. For some reason, the first and the last day of a trip always seems stressful. I rarely sleep well either day. It's the getting in and getting out that causes all the problems. On the way in, I'm always worrying about the little things: flights, luggage, transportation, accommodations, guides, wind and rain, and most of all, my customers. On the way out, I'm anxious to get home as soon as possible. Somewhere around four o'clock, I woke up again. This time I stayed up, took a shower, and made some coffee. Finally,

I loaded the golf cart and took my gear to the docks. I was the first in line, and for some reason, I felt better about the day. It was time to leave, time to go home.

While we enjoyed another outstanding breakfast, the guides were busy loading our gear in the skiffs. A few minutes later, we said our goodbyes and jumped in the skiffs for the short run to Grand Bahama Island. We reached the airport early enough for the film crew to deal with customs and immigrations. Of course, they had to grease a few more palms. That was to be expected; after all, it was the Bahamas. When we landed in Fort Lauderdale, we shook hands. We gave each other a bear hug or two, and then parted ways. A few hours later, I was home. And it was good to be home.

The Windswept Beaches of the Yucatán

SEVERAL MONTHS AFTER MY LAST TRIP TO BELIZE, I WAS ABOUT TO take a group of eleven fly fishermen down to Pesca Maya to chase permit for seven days. At the time, Pesca Maya was a quaint little fishing lodge nestled in a stand of windswept palm trees just north of Punta Allen, the jumping-off point for some of the best permit fishing in the Yucatán. Coastal green shrubs choke the beaches, a litany of herbaceous plants perfume the sea breeze, and a few hardy trees manage to scratch out a living in the sandy soil. Scattered throughout the landscape, you can find orchids, bromeliads, and an astonishing array of other flowering plants of which I do not know the names but find pretty nonetheless. On the bayside, dense mangrove islands host aquatic nurseries that reign high among the most prolific in the southern hemisphere.

As misfortune would have it, a week before we were scheduled to leave, a Category 4 hurricane named Wilma came barreling out of the Caribbean and swept across the upper Yucatán Peninsula. Then, as if that hadn't been enough destruction for one go, the cyclone picked up speed, made a U-turn, spiraled north by northeast, and swept across southwest Florida. Having experienced the aftermath of my fair share of hurricanes, I tried everything to convince my customers to postpone the trip and give the owner time to repair the damages to the lodge. But it didn't matter how much I pleaded. No one wanted to move the trip to a later date. At the time, putting up with a little damage struck my customers as a small price to pay for the opportunity to catch a permit on the fly.

Later that day, the lodge owner called and reassured me the repairs were minor and the lodge would be up and running in the next several days. Such self-assured prescience should have required borrowing the seeing-stone, Palantir, from Saruman, the White Wizard of Isengard. I also realized that late in September, the hurricane season was not over; the chance of another late-season cyclone remained. El Niño's tantrums still had the potential to wreak havoc in the Pacific. For lack of a better name, local fishermen had christened the weather pattern El Niño as El Niño de Navidad ("the Christ child"), presumably because its effects peaked around Christmas. La Niña ("the little girl") can have the same deleterious effect on the climate but in reverse. Rarely, if ever, does either of these temperamental children positively impact the fishing on the East Coast. In short, as long as we were still under an El Niño, extreme weather in the Gulf of Mexico remained in play.

Not totally convinced of the lodge owner's assertions, to say the least, I did my best to invoke the power of positive thinking since, upon my customers' insistence, we were headed south to the Yucatán with or without my blessing. A week later, we took to the skies. Most of my clients did not share the same flights; their flights were scheduled to arrive at different times throughout the day. Anybody with travel experience in the Caribbean can attest to the chronic unreliability of arrival and departure times. Cancún is a tourist destination and a jumping-off point for dozens of cruise lines, not to mention hundreds of beach resorts lining the Yucatán. Depending on how many planes are taxiing to get on the runway and how many planes are in a holding pattern in the sky, posted departure times do not necessarily determine which plane gets to take off or land. The aircraft circling above, slowly running out of gas, understandably get first dibs at any runway slot opening up. In short, many passengers are treated to aerial tours of the Cancún airport for long stretches of time.

When your lucky number is drawn and your plane finally lands, you are not out of the airport chaos yet. The airport from which you are arriving, the number of connections that make up your itinerary, and the time of day at which you arrive dictate how long it will take to get from the tarmac to the baggage claim. If you happen to land midday, you have to deal with long lines of angry tourists not always on their best behavior (and I am being incredibly kind). As the day drags on, the runway begins to look like the Macy's Thanksgiving Day Parade on steroids, and the terminal has the look and feel of Bourbon Street on Fat Tuesday, which might sound like fun except that you still have to clear customs and immigration.

Fortunately, my flight was a hop, skip, and jump from Mobile, and I snuck in before the hubbub started. I still had to wait for the gathering of the tribe though. The day began like a slow drip, but eventually everyone arrived, most in a somewhat grumpy mood. Although the sight outside the airport doors proved somewhat encouraging with regard to my fears of devastation from natural disaster, Cancún looked like what you would expect in a city that recently stood tall in the face of a Category 4 hurricane and survived: ragged in places but somewhat functional in others. Then again, we still needed to make the long march south toward Punta Allen, the land of permit, Mayan guides, pangas, and the all-important tiki bar.

Serving as host and quasi guide, I wanted to put a bright face on the circumstances and give the lodge owner the benefit of the doubt in believing that the Dodge van he provided was large enough for twelve fishermen, one guide, a driver, and our luggage, but I couldn't. The lodge owner must have thought we were twelve Halflings, not twelve adults. Somehow we all did manage to squeeze in. Unfortunately, I must have forgotten to put on the trip list that comfortable attire for the tropics consists of summer whites, short sleeves, and short pants. It had not occurred to me that someone would show up in long pants and a long-sleeved shirt, although it has been my experience that people tend to dress for the climate from which they hail, rarely for the environment in which they intend to fish. On the other hand, I wore shorts, a T-shirt, a Miami Dolphins baseball hat, and flip-flops.

After a long, agonizing trip south (during which the driver predictably felt the irresistible need to stop at multiple tourist-trap road stands), we finally pulled up in front of the lodge. As the guide opened the side door and we started crawling out of the sardine can the lodge called a van, the quiet was deafening. You could have heard the footfalls of a banded gecko making its way across the porch. My customers looked mortified; the lodge was anything but ready for business. First, I noticed the tiki bar was gone (maybe because I had just about reached the point where I needed a stiff drink). Next, the large number of Federales walking up and down the beach caught my eye. I assumed they were Federales; then again, it might have been the Mexican military. If I had to venture a guess as to the purpose of this "nature walk," I would wager they were looking for illicit drugs scattered along the beaches from Wilma, but then again, what the hell do I know? To my shame (and my wife's continual berating), the only two phrases of Spanish I can muster, even after having successfully completed two semesters of it in college, are *cómo estás, señorita* and *mucho cerveza*, both of which I learned from the Jimmy Buffett album *Son of a Son of a Sailor*.

Ian, the lodge manager, greeted my shell-shocked crew and delivered the warmly reassuring news that the lodge owner had been called away on family business but was sure to turn up in the next few days or so. Ian then treated us to a brief tour of the damages and assured us that the air-conditioning should be up and running posthaste. But, of course, he meant to say that the air-conditioning should be up and running the day after we checked out. Finally, the guides dragged our luggage to our assigned rooms. As they were leaving, they smiled and told us "not to leave our bags on the floor and to constantly check our shoes before putting them on." Travel is educational; that day, we learned that scorpions love to hide in dark places, and we learned it well.

The news kept getting better; later that evening, one of the guides whispered into my ear that the cook and his wife had pitched a hissy fit and walked out several days ago. Evidently, the chef had informed the manager that he had no intention of coming back unless the owner offered him a substantial raise. Bottom line, until the owner capitulated, the guides were in charge of all the cooking. I chose not to share that information with my customers, figuring they had already been given enough to digest for one travel day.

To my surprise, a few of the guides' wives and kids showed up and saved the day. The Spanish paella they created proved excellent. When it came to dessert, I admit I am not a fan of the flan, but I don't remember any leftovers. Quite the opposite: I recall the other guests scraping the porcelain off the dinner plates as if they were trying to see what was on the other side. Rounding out the evening, the margaritas started to flow around nightfall. We learned something else that night: North of the border but south of the Mason-Dixon Line, a margarita consists of three parts tequila, two parts triple sec (or agave), one freshly squeezed lime, and salt for the glass. They have a slightly different version in the Yucatán. The ratios are five parts tequila, one part triple sec, and throw away the lime. If nothing else, cut the lime into wedges, drop it in the margarita to soak, and eat the lime when the glass is empty. To say that we slithered away from the dinner table that night would be an understatement. Like Loretta Lynn's song, "Don't Come Home a Drinkin'." The next day, we knew last night got drunk.

The evening had turned into a hard day's night, and sunrise was right below the horizon. I spent the next hour rigging three fly rods: a ten-weight for permit, a nine-weight for tarpon, and an eight-weight for snook. Following that, I grabbed half a dozen fly boxes, stuffed them in my dry bag, hung up my clothes, put my flip-flops on the coat rack, and crawled into bed. Two hours later, I was sitting at the makeshift bar having a cup of coffee and talking shop with the guides. I wanted them to know that I had no intention of chasing the overgrown pilchards the Mayan guides called bonefish, but had come to chase permit. For some reason that seemed to elevate my status in the eyes of our guides and to afford me certain privileges and considerations.

The trip had officially begun.

Breakfast was at seven sharp. I was beginning to think I was the only one who had decided to have breakfast. I admit my stomach might have been a little queasy from all the food and the occasional margarita last night, but why should I let something as mundane as a hangover get in the way of possibly catching a permit on the fly? Then I heard a booming voice resonating through the dining room. It was Bill Bentley, a unique individual, I must say. When Bill and his wife Kathy showed up at the airport, their entire luggage for the trip consisted of one over-the-shoulder travel bag about the size of a small briefcase. From what the other guests had told me, the Bentleys were somewhat wealthy, traveled extensively worldwide, and rarely carried anything except two changes of clothes and a few toiletries.

Since Bill didn't bring any fishing gear, I was somewhat interested in what he was going to fish with or, conversely, what he intended to catch without any gear. Still, after I had finished my breakfast and started heading to the docks, I was more than happy to share the panga with Bill, who seemed to be the only other fisherman interested in going out that morning. When we reached what looked like an old wooden scow, we saw our guide, Fabio, stuffing an armload of spinning rods under a makeshift gunwale. I took a deep breath and sighed. Somehow, Bill had convinced the guide to scavenge some old gear for him, apparently the stuff left by a previous customer. The sun was starting to climb over the palm trees, and the temperature rose at about an equal rate. Although it was still reasonably cool, there wasn't a cloud in the sky, and even though the humidity seemed to be low, the sweat had already commenced beading on my brow. Of course, it was only a trickle at this stage, but it was a harbinger of what we had to look forward to for the next six days.

Being the caring kind of host, I even went as far as to surrender the bow of the boat to any of my fishing compañeros to chase bonefish, except for those short moments when tailing permit or a mudding stingray covered with permit was in sight. I also had a heart-to-heart with the guide, endeavoring to make him understand that we wanted to ensure Bill had the opportunity to catch as many bonefish as he could. As much as I wanted to catch a permit, I wanted Bill to have a wonderful time. Some might say that's a canard of sorts, but on the other hand, that's why the gods created the sun and the moon, which give us four tides: two ebbing tides for bonefish and two flood tides to chase permit.

We idled away from the dock, heading mostly north and hanging tight to the coastline. It had been years since I had fished Pesca Maya, and if not for the sun, I wouldn't have had any idea in what direction we were headed. The thousands of mangrove islands really do start to look alike after a few hours on the water. Nevertheless, it wasn't difficult to see that Fabio knew his way in and around the backcountry.

Most, if not all, of the Mayan guides started their fishing careers as commercial fishermen who eventually worked their way up the totem pole to become fishing guides. Most of them became excellent guides. It occurred to me that most of the guides in the fishing villages throughout

Central America are related to each other, and why not? There is no other way to support your wife and kids other than the thriving eco-tourism business or the local resorts. Most of the guides in the Yucatán speak Spanglish, but there are a number of different dialects, including one named Bajacaliforniense. So I like to tell my wife that even if I had retained more of my college Spanish, taught with a decidedly Georgia-Southern-US accent, it would not have helped me much in conversing with our guides in their native tongue.

The Yucatán and Central American guides tend to distinguish themselves as being exceptionally hardworking. Depending on how well you get to know them, they will stay on the water with you until you have had every opportunity to catch whatever your quarry might be. The truth is that the best guides I have fished with would much prefer to be on the water than back at the lodge, and if you treat them with courtesy, they will do almost anything for you. Sadly, not all clients seem to understand that.

We ran hard for the next twenty minutes before making a wide turn to port. Then Fabio shut the engine down and climbed up on the poling platform. It didn't take but an instant for him to point far back into the estuary, where hundreds of bonefish tails gleamed in the bright sunlight. His suggestion was we get out of the panga and wade.

It doesn't matter if you are fishing out of a shiny new Hell's Bay or a run-down panga held together with duct tape (both have their advantages and disadvantages, especially for someone who hasn't spent much time in the brine). Standing on the deck of a flats boat gives the fisherman a distinct height advantage, but the hatch port cover swings both ways—it's equally easy for bonefish to see you. On the other hand, wading allows the angler to creep up on the bonefish without spooking them, though it requires stealth and the patience of a monastic monk, which few fishermen seem to have. But wading a pristine flat smothered in turtle grass in the middle of the Yucatán is, at some level, a spiritual experience. If the conditions are favorable, wading the flats by yourself or with a guide can be entertaining, if not educational, especially if you choose to wade barefoot.

If the reader is wondering, yes, I have suffered a few painful repercussions for this folly here and there: I have stubbed my toes more times than I care to recall, and I stepped on a sea urchin once, which turned out to be a nightmare. My foot swelled up to the size of a small football. Visiting Los Roques one time, I was wading one of the pancake flats that the locale is famous for while fighting a six- or seven-pound bonefish, when a lemon shark chased said bonefish between my legs. The lemon shark's pectoral fins carved up both my inner calf muscles. The water turned various shades of red, my fly rod exploded into three pieces, and fortunately for the bonefish, my tippet popped like a worn-out guitar string. However, the latter incident would have happened regardless of whether I waded barefoot or in boots.

Although not averse to wading per se, I didn't want to spend the next several hours chasing ten- or twelve-inch bonefish. So I asked Fabio if I could float the panga out to the edge of the channel and anchor up while he was trying to put Bill on his first bonefish. His eyes grew to the size of small saucers, but after asking me a few obvious questions about boatmanship, he acquiesced graciously. I had no real intention of fishing; I just wanted to anchor up and see what might swim by the old scow. Looking back, it's incredible to think how much of my life has been spent staring into the abyss, either looking for fish or just watching the tide run by. But if I happened to bump into a permit working its way up the edge of the flat, who could blame me if I made a few casts?

Even though the old scow belonged to Fabio, I was the master and commander at this moment. Granted, it was a small ship, but a ship nonetheless. I headed out onto the vast flat smothered in turtle grass. An enormous mangrove forest, awash in dark greens, sheltered the flat on one side. The reflection of the early morning sun bouncing off the white sand remained blinding even through a good pair of sunglasses. I was gently bobbing along in Fabio's panga when I realized that life was but a dream, like Lewis Carroll's *Alice's Adventure in Wonderland*. I admit to experiencing a bit of a John Denver moment: corny to the highest degree but life-affirming and soul-nourishing as heck.

The Yucatán is a bird-watcher's paradise. Five hundred and sixty-five species of birds call that area of the Gulf of Mexico home. Maybe the most interesting is the dark red flamingo, the Yucatán's most beloved bird, in addition to the vast number of parrots you find in the jungles.

Given the opportunity, I could spend an entire day just watching white pelicans and various herons making a living in and around the estuaries. The Yucatán remains one of the most remarkable ecosystems left on the planet. Unfortunately, like every other intact ecosystem on earth, civilization is creeping in at an alarming pace. At one time, only a handful of fishing lodges dotted the coast from Cancún to Tulum. Now, between the hordes of fishermen and the cruise ships, many of these places have lost nearly all their charm. Everyone is trying to make a buck off the influx of tourists. Paradoxically, we humans don't seem to care much about the ecosystems we claim to love and pay good money to visit.

Conservationist Archie Carr once opined, "For most of the wild things on earth, the future must depend on the conscience of mankind." Archie knew it would require more than just a village of dedicated naturalists and volunteers to save what was left; it would require a paradigm shift in the way humans think about the natural world. To save what's left of Archie's vision, we would eventually have to protect the remaining flora and fauna for the planet's sake, and not necessarily for human pleasure and convenience.

Speaking of inconvenience and local fauna, I could see Fabio and Bill working their way across the flats, but between the white pelicans paddling around in the potholes looking for breakfast and the gray pelicans dive-bombing the schools of juvenile bonefish, I didn't see them getting close enough to their quarry to make a decent cast using a wiggle jig. The wiggle jig was first tied in the Florida Keys over fifty years ago. (Well, at least that was the first time I fished one.) Every time I go to a trade show these days, I run into someone who claims to have invented the damn thing. I have no idea who tied the first wiggle jig, but Phillips Fly and Tackle Company in Pennsylvania filed the first patent on April 9, 1979. I remember first using one in the late 1960s on the ocean-side flats off Big Pine Key. Considering the patent date, that seems improbable, but who knows, Phillips may have just waited ten years to patent the thing. The point is, it remains hands-down the best bonefish jig tied in the northern hemisphere. The wiggle jig also works well on small tarpon and permit. But like all bonefish jigs, it still requires an accurate cast and a little patience on the angler's part.

In the distance, I could see Bill walking around in circles, surrounded by schools of bonefish that were probably having a good laugh at him. Every time Bill thought he had the opportunity to cast to one, he missed by fifteen feet or more. It wasn't difficult to see that Bill was new to flats fishing. I could hear him cussing from several hundred yards away. Fabio was trying his best to calm Bill down, but I could see Bill had a better chance of landing a bonefish by randomly throwing rocks than his "precision" casting of hand-me-down gear. He didn't strike me as the kind of man who would tolerate getting skunked, not even if by his own fault. So I poled the panga back up on the flat, grabbed a fly rod, crawled over the gunwale, and slowly made my way over to Fabio. By that time, Bill had pounded the water into froth. Fabio was mumbling something in Spanish as I walked up and handed him the fly rod, suggesting that he try showing Bill how much easier it would be if he learned how to use a fly rod.

To my surprise, Bill did know. He lived in Idaho and had fished with a fly rod since he was a kid growing up on his family's ranch outside Coeur d'Alene. The obvious question remained: Why didn't Bill bring a fly rod, or at least borrow one? When we made it back to the panga, I asked him why he wasted so much time using a spinning rod when he could have used one of my fly rods. The answer was easy. Bill hated carrying rod tubes and reel cases and all the other paraphernalia that fly fishermen lugged around. I asked Fabio to head back to the lodge for lunch so that I could rig up a few fly rods for Bill. In the back of my mind, I contemplated the other alternative: Bill, back at the lodge, and let one of the other guides deal with him. I have a hunch that a similar thought crossed Fabio's mind.

When we reached the lodge, it was almost empty. We spent a few minutes looking around for the other guests. To our surprise, we were apprised that the other fishermen had somehow managed to crawl out of bed, eat a late breakfast, and then go fishing. According to one of the housekeepers, they had seemed a little under the weather but still kicking. That information had the benefit of reassuring me as host. The absence of other fishermen dashed our selfless concept of mixing up boatmates and guides to diversify the fishing experience and allow friendships to blossom.

While Fabio brought the lunches up from the panga so we could indulge in a leisurely meal in the dining room, I went to my room to collect a seven-weight and a rather heavy nine-weight with floating lines and shooting heads for Bill. After a hearty lunch and a brief siesta, Fabio and I decided to do whatever it might take to put Bill on a few bonefish. We were both in agreement that if we didn't do our best to put him on some fish, we would never live it down.

So, I tied a Crazy Charlie on for Bill. The lucky recipient just stared at it for a few minutes, inducing me to inquire if he knew how to double haul. I might as well have been speaking in Archaic Latin. Then, realizing that it would be a long afternoon, I mentioned to Fabio that we needed to find a shallow flat and spend some time with Bill before blowing up any more bonefish schools. It didn't take long before Fabio beached the panga on a nearby flat. The white-sand flat seemed to go on for miles, and even though the tide was coming in, our flat remained relatively shallow. Clear, shallow water meant good visibility, which provided the added benefit that, if we accidentally ran into a school of bonefish, Bill could observe how they move in synchronous motion with one another and just how spooky they can be when they perceive a threat.

Fabio and I flipped a quarter to see which one of us would start the tutorial. Not because we expected Bill to be a difficult student, given that he already knew how to cast and swing streamers for trout, but because whoever lost the coin toss had to spend the next several hours standing in the sun, patiently teaching Bill how to stalk, cast, and land a bonefish. Whoever won could enjoy kicking back in the panga under a shady mangrove, downing a few cervezas.

Fabio smiled and offered me a beer as I climbed out of the panga. I smiled back like a good sport; after all, fly-fishing instruction is also part of what I do for a living. That's why they pay me the big bucks, right? But, on the other hand, that's why I pay Fabio the bigger bucks. Fabio settled in to earn them by leaning against the poling platform, drinking cerveza, and shouting occasional pearls of wisdom for moral support.

Through such "combined" tutelage, Bill improved notably, making a few casts at the occasional bonefish. But, if it were easy to pick up in an afternoon, there'd be no fun in it. Also, like most of us learning a new variation of something at which we consider ourselves experts otherwise, Bill clearly needed some tough love. I never knew if he was serious about learning how to fish the flats or if he thought the exercise futile. In any event, I decided that the job of stating some harsh truths should fall squarely at the feet of the fishing guide and not the fishing partner, and certainly not the trip host.

That night over dinner, the guests regaled each other with tales of the day's fishing; some had experienced great days, others had various levels of less success. I didn't hear anybody complaining either way, not even Bill, to my highest elation. The truth is, Bill needed to be standing on the bow of the panga making short casts. As on the first day, that's how it went for the next several days. Some guests preferred to fish out of the pangas; some liked to be in the water stalking the fish up close and personal; and others, like me, burned holes in the water looking for permit.

When I was a kid growing up in South Florida, we fished the channels in the upper keys for what we called tideline permit. The outgoing tide flushed a tremendous amount of grass out of the backcountry. The grass was thick with shrimp and crabs. Depending on the contour of the mouth of the pass, permit stacked up in huge numbers and gorged themselves on a smorgasbord of various crustaceans. We would float out with the tide and pitch pass crabs to the permit. It was as easy as taking candy from a baby. On the other hand, trying to fool them with an artificial fly seemed like a waste of time and energy. Fortunately for us, a similar situation can be found in the Yucatán—not necessarily at the mouth of the passes, but deep in the backcountry. There, in the deep channels between two extensive flats, on the outgoing tides, you can find something that at least looks and feels familiar.

Depending on the stage of the outgoing tide and the depth of the channel, you still have to maneuver the fly in front of the permit. Permit move up and down the water column looking for food. Often they stack up at the bottom of the channel and move from side to side. In other words, putting the fly immediately in front of the permit is a little tricky.

However, having mastered that feat, the only tiny issue that remains is the near impossibility of fooling one with a fly. The clarity of the water can be your friend or not. If the water is crystal clear, the fish can be incredibly spooky, and if the water is murky, it isn't easy to spot the fish. The fluctuating speed of the tide doesn't help either. A wiser person would simply find more cooperative fish on the ocean-side flats, but where's the fun in that?

It should be evident to the reader that, with our trip nearing its end, I am trying to find justification for me not having hooked a permit. Then again, the end of a trip often holds the most promise. The first two or three days of any fishing trip can be stressful until everybody has the local routine down pat. On the other hand, the last several days can be cosmic: The lodge starts to feel like a home away from home. You know the guides and their family like they were your next-door neighbors and, for the most part, have already tripped over whatever hidden surprises the trip has to offer. Toward the end, it feels as though the fishing improves, when the fishermen are the ones who are actually improving. We start spotting fish even before the guide, and that twenty-foot cast that seemed almost impossible four days prior pales in comparison to the forty- and fifty-foot casts we are booming out at the end of the trip.

I promised another customer, David, that we would spend the last several days on the water together. David loves to chase bonefish; he doesn't care if he never saw another permit in his life. Sometime in the past, David had spent years trying to catch a permit on the fly and, for whatever reason, never managed to get one to participate. It's a familiar tale. Permit are uncooperative little buggers. The upshot of David's lack of interest in permit was that we formed a great team; he enjoyed fishing for bonefish, while I scoured the flats for permit.

On our fateful last day, Fabio suggested we head south. Far off in the distance, we could make out colossal cumulus clouds looking like billowing cotton balls. Such clouds are considered fair-weather clouds in the tropics. In another hour or so, the tide would be at full flood, and if we were lucky, the bonefish and permit would be easing their way into the labyrinth of the multitudes of small mangrove islands that surrounded the flats we wanted to fish. Fabio shut down the engine almost a quarter mile from the flat, grabbed the push pole, and climbed up on the poling platform. It was easy poling. Fabio was smart enough to use the incoming tide to his advantage. It might have taken a few extra minutes to get there, but we avoided spooking any fish along the way. We floated up on the flat and waited for half an hour. The last thing we wanted to do was run the fish off the flats. It was starting to get hot, and the sun's reflection off the water was blinding. We could have circumnavigated the flats and came in from the south, but Fabio was trying to maximize our time on what could easily be considered the best tide of the day. When the time was right, David stripped out thirty or forty feet of fly line on the deck, made a few false casts, then restacked his fly line from bottom to top so the line would come off the deck without tangling. While he was thus occupied, I reiterated our solemn agreement: The bonefish were all his, but it'd be my turn to cast if we spotted a permit. David laughed and mumbled something like, "You can have them all."

As the sun climbed higher, rendering the temperature nigh unbearable, Fabio slowly poled the panga into the maze of dense mangroves. "Bonefish at ten o'clock, about seventy feet out," Fabio whispered when he spotted a small school of a half-dozen tails making their way into the mangroves. From what I could make out, they looked like three- or four-pound bones (anything over three pounds in the Yucatán is considered enormous). Getting one to take a fly was the easy part. Making a great cast in the middle of the dense mangroves would require skill. Everywhere you looked, giant mangroves blocked the airways. Fabio suggested that David leave the boat to see how close he could approach without spooking the fish. So David slid over the gunwale as quietly as he could muster and did his best to sneak up on the bonefish. He might have stood a better chance if the wind had been blowing hard enough to ripple the water's surface. As it was, nothing prevented the fish from noticing us as clearly as we saw them. As a result, when David took one step, the school of bonefish took two. It was as if they could feel the pressure every time David took a step. Finally, he grew so frustrated that he just made a long, spirited cast. When his fly hit the water, the fish exploded in all directions.

The fun (mostly the fish's) continued in vain for the next several hours. Eventually, we floated deep into the maze, where Fabio recommended that David tie on a small tarpon fly. The reason became apparent when the thick mangrove tunnel we had been easing through opened up into a rather large lake; tarpon rolled everywhere. We tarried there for the next hour, jumping one small tarpon after another. It was fun, despite the sweltering heat.

As the tide started to drop, Fabio impressed upon us the need to return to open water, as this was the last place you wanted to get stuck in the mud and muck at low tide. Consequently, we floated out with the tide, leaving our friends the tarpon behind. Half an hour later, we were poling our way south along the outside of the flat when I noticed a giant mud and a huge tail waving in the air as if to say hello. It could have easily been the largest mudding permit I had ever laid eyes on, and only seventy feet away, give or take a few inches. What's more, the massive permit appeared utterly oblivious to our panga. Excited, I told David to get his line back on the reel as I stripped mine off my Tibor. The plan was to drop a Merkin Crab directly on the permit's head once I had enough line to make my cast.

Fabio did his part, slowly inching the panga closer. On the other hand, David appeared so mesmerized by the big permit that he needed to be reminded by both Fabio and me to switch positions and drop his rod so I could climb onto the bow to make a decent cast. By this time, we had arrived within roughly twenty-five feet of the permit. David picked up his rod off the deck and started inching his way closer and closer to the bow for a look.

I yelled, "Duck!" I was going to make the cast even if I had to make it directly over his head.

However, the splash I heard next was not from my fly hitting the water; rather, it was associated with the disappearance of one fiddle-footed fly fisher falling off the bow of the boat. David had walked right off the end of the panga, falling squarely on top of the permit. The fish took off with a vengeance while David started flailing in all directions as if fighting for his life. This desperate struggle continued until Fabio made the not illogical suggestion that David might try standing up. I must have taken dozens of photos of David splashing in the mud until he finally managed to get back on his feet, at which point he stood submerged in a generous two and a half feet of water.

Possibly in an attempt to butter me up so I would delete the photos, David apologized dozens of times on the way back to the lodge. I ignored his none-too-subtle inquiries about my intentions regarding those snapshots. Considerate host that I am, I certainly harbored no intentions of passing them around the dinner table that night. That, to me, sounded like a job for the wife, because I know mine would. My hunch regarding spousal collaboration was reaffirmed when we arrived back to the dock, where David's wife was enjoying margaritas with a few friends at the makeshift bar. As soon as David climbed out of the panga, his dearly beloved broke out in laughter. There he stood, the love of her life, covered from head to toe in dark, sticky muck. All the belongings he carried off the boat sported an equally liberal coating. Caught brown-handed, what choice did poor David have but to regale the assembled masses with his near-death adventure. I noticed that he put his spin on the story, and that every time he told the story, it changed a little. By the end of the night, most considered him a hero. I, on the other hand, considered him the Antichrist.

After that misadventure, we had one last day of fishing left. The last day of a fishing trip takes on its own character. Not everyone likes to fish on the final day; some want to go into town and spend a few bucks or visit local attractions. Others like to party a little too much the night before, sleep in the last day and use it to pack at their leisure, to avoid feeling rushed the following morning. On the other hand, I like to pack the night before, then sneak out early with a guide and fish till I drop. Often it's the only chance I get to spend the day on the bow of the panga. Sometimes I arrange to stay an extra day and fish with the owner, though more often than not the day is spent talking shop.

Access to the boat's bow the last day did me little good. We spotted a few smaller permit here and there, but nothing like the giant of the previous day, nor did any of his friends or family members bother to show up. So the trip ended without me having had the chance to cast to a permit, but to take a page out of the gambler's handbook, there is always next time.

We had breakfast at the lodge the following day, piled into the cramped van, and made the hot, uncomfortable drive back to the airport. Since I hate to be rushed on the return trip, I usually book my flights home a little later in the afternoon or evening. It also allows me some time to spend with my customers before they have to board, helping them navigate the airport with as little stress as possible, reminiscing about the fun days spent, and perhaps planning for our next trip.

Fifty Ways to Lose a Permit

ON THE FLIGHT HOME, I BEGAN TO QUESTION THE SANITY OF SPENDING so much time and energy, not to mention money, trying to catch a fish that's so damn difficult to catch. Granted, it's not impossible to catch a permit on a fly, but for most fly fishermen, it's challenging, so challenging that most move on after their first or second attempt. I always thought travel in itself should be worth the price of admission, especially if you happen to be fishing the Yucatán or any Central American country that skirts the Atlantic.

I was wrong on so many levels. The majority of the fishermen I've fished with over the years are interested in one thing, and one thing only, a permit on the fly.

Catching and landing a permit on the fly requires, if nothing else, a good sense of humor. I, for one, am not ready to admit that a permit is more intelligent than I am, although it may appear that way sometimes. All it takes is a positive attitude and the patience of a gopher tortoise.

Unfortunately, some fishermen find it challenging to chill out and enjoy the moment regardless, whether it's a family vacation or a fishing trip. Occasionally, I run into the odd fisherman who's wired even tighter than a permit. Spending a few hours at the pool or on the beach downing margaritas is out of the question. Exploring the mangrove forest and taking a tour of the local ruins can wait until next year. To most fly fishermen, the mangrove forest is just a bunch of trees and shrubs full of mosquitoes, but to the estuaries, the forest is essential to the health and well-being of all living creatures that call the mangroves home. In essence, the mangroves are responsible for the turtle grass, and without the turtle grass, you wouldn't have any flats, and without the flats, you wouldn't have any bonefish and permit. Then you'd be back at the same old tiki bar downing the same old margaritas you turned your nose up to a week earlier.

I think two things cause it. One is the lack of understanding of something called the gestalt theory, which means the whole is greater than the sum of all its parts. Essentially it means the total experience of the trip is more important than catching a permit on the fly. Second is the inability to slow down and smell the proverbial roses. It took me years to catch my first permit on a fly, and even then, the permit came reluctantly. Sometimes it's a hard pill to swallow, considering how much you paid for the trip. Permit fishing can be expensive, but the price of the trip has little to do with your success rate.

If you like to spend your free time staked out on a pristine flat somewhere in the Yucatán, knee-deep in turtle grass, you need to jump on the bandwagon and help save what's left of the magnificent mangrove forests that protect the flats you love to fish. More important than catching a permit on the fly is protecting the environments where the permit lives. Almost all the estuaries from the tip of the Yucatán to Los Roques and throughout the Caribbean are under assault from rabid development, commercial fishing, pollution, overpopulation, and loss of habitat, to name a few. It's a problem facing most watersheds and ecosystems. If fishermen don't become stewards of the environment, we will lose everything we hold dear to our hearts.

Suffice it to say that catching a permit on the fly gets more difficult as the years pass. And I have to admit I have lost considerably more permit than I have caught. Even though I have no actual data to back up my thesis, most fishermen would agree that it's exponentially better to have loved and lost than never loved in the first place. To love, you has to play the field, regardless of whether you are chasing a ladyfish or a thirty-pound permit. To lose fifty permit, you has to stalk and hook at least that many. Regardless of your experience, you will likely catch a few along the way, or at the very least spot enough to motivate you to continue your quest to catch a permit on the fly. So the question becomes, are there fifty ways to lose a permit? Although I have never actually counted the number of ways I have lost a permit, I would have to say yes, maybe even more.

Over the years, I have spoken to countless fly fishermen, young and old, who have dreamed of catching a permit on a fly. To my consternation, very few fishermen have intentionally gone looking for one, much less pitched a fly to a permit. Most have run across one or two here and there while fishing for bonefish or tarpon. Once in a blue moon, a permit will cross over to the dark side and pick up a bonefish fly or pounce on a small tarpon fly. For most of us, that's how the adventure began, like Alice and the damn rabbit hole—out of control and blind as a bat with absolutely no idea how to get back.

Most fly fishermen spend an inordinate amount of time with their snout buried in books written by other fishermen who may or may not have any motivation to share their success. Most have read about how difficult it is to hook and land a permit on the fly. Then, without any objective evidence, they buy into the propaganda spread by other fishermen—hook, line, and sinker. I am not saying that other writers would intentionally mislead the novice permit fisherman. On the other hand, I am not saying they wouldn't at least send you astray on a muddy flat that hasn't seen a permit since the Paleozoic era some 541 million years ago. After all, there are only so many permit. And a good permit flat is hard to come by these days, and the last thing fishermen need is more competition.

Face it, the learning curve for catching a permit on the fly is rather steep at first. For the most part, it takes a relatively skilled angler to stalk, cast, hook, and land one. Therein lies the dilemma; it takes time on the water to hone these skills. Even then, it helps to solicit the tutelage of a skilled guide. Of course it also doesn't hurt to have access to productive permit flats. Regardless of how much time and energy you expend, fly-fishing for permit in Alaska can be a somewhat fruitless and futile exercise. Sadly, unless you happen to live in the Caribbean or the Florida Keys, you are unlikely to have access to permit in your backyard. On the bright side, those are not the worst places to have to visit for frequent practice runs. Even the family usually likes such vacation spots, which allows for clever repackaging of a fishing trip as a family excursion for the spouse and children. Of course, you're not fooling anyone but yourself. Your spouse and kids know exactly what you're doing, but I've found it's a small price to pay for the opportunity to sneak out on a mangrove flat smothered in turtle grass and stalk a few permit before breakfast.

I count myself as one of the privileged few to grow up in the heyday of the Miami Metropolitan Fishing Tournament, better known as the MET and once considered the preeminent fishing tournament on the planet. It's difficult to say which game species sat at the top of the pantheon of gods of the ancient Mayans, but one of if not the most coveted fish at the MET was the permit. Nevertheless, until Del Brown invented Del's Merkin Crab (some know it as Del's Brown Crab Fly), catching a permit on the fly was considered almost impossible, at the very least extremely difficult. Nevertheless, Del managed to hoodwink over 300 permit in his lifetime, depending on whom you ask. Others will tell you he caught precisely 513 permit on the fly. On the other hand, I have caught exactly 14 permit on the fly, and 11 of them have been hooked and landed on some version of the Merkin Crab.

Eventually, I took up fly fishing and expanded to flies instead of crabs. That's not to say I never use crabs, because I do. In fact, in certain circumstances, a small crab is almost the only way to entice a permit when the wind is blowing directly in your face at thirty-five miles an hour. Face it, the tropics are the tropics because of the intense winds and rain. It's something you have to come to terms with at some point. If not, you might find yourself spending a tremendous amount of time at the tiki bar knocking back rumrunners topped with a Myers floater. Then again, if pitching live crabs to permit offends your sensibilities, there is always windsurfing. I hear it's a lot of fun.

Unfortunately, like most things in life, permit have a way of getting under your skin. It's like Papa winning the Nobel Prize for *The Old Man and the Sea*. You wake up one day, and you find yourself too old or too damn drunk to accept the prize.

In the not-too-distant past, I spent considerable time at Deep Water Cay chasing bonefish and permit. Depending on the time of year and the weather, the fishing was fantastic. The flats southeast of Deep Water Cay held an astonishing number of permit on the incoming tides, and catching one or two a day was considered doable, not impossible, for the experienced fly fisherman. In September 2019, Hurricane Dorian ripped my heart out. The powerful cyclone barreled down on Deep Water Cay like a runaway locomotive and scoured it clean like a well-seasoned cast-iron skillet. Ownership immediately shut down all operations, and according to owner Paul Vahldiek, he has no intentions of rebuilding.

The somewhat inconvenient truth is that nowadays, one must travel a fair distance to encounter permit. The Florida Keys still have their share of permit but can be crowded at times. The going rates for guides and lodging stagger the imagination. Often I'm asked where is the best place to chase permit. Perhaps more apropos is where is the best place to *catch* a permit. Nearly as important as location is the time of year, the tides, the phase of the moon (which dictates the tides and may be different depending on the location), and finally, the lodge. The better the decisions you make about these details, the better the chances are of actually catching a permit rather than standing on the bow of the boat staring into the abyss just hoping and praying a permit swims by and waves at you.

Permit traditionally spawn in April, May, June, and July in deep water, not necessarily in shallow water, where you will find guides throughout the Caribbean and Central America looking for permit. I'm flying by the seat of my pants here, because they're just now ramping up the research, and it seems that every time I open up my mouth, I am proven wrong at some level. I am not saying you can't run across a permit any time of the year, but considering how much it costs to chase a permit, one does like to stack the odds in one's favor, and not all pocketbooks are created equal. I have to admit I have seen permit up on the flats almost every month of the year. That's not to say that some months are inherently better than others. The best advice I can conjure up is to do your homework. It has always paid dividends for my fishing buddies and me.

I have caught more than my share of permit using conventional gear. But, more often than not, I am fishing with someone else, with or without a guide. Traditionally my fishing partner is standing on the bow, ready to strike at a moment's notice. If we are fishing with a guide, he usually points out the fish, then barks out the direction and distance. Nothing in the world gets the blood boiling like the words "ten o'clock, permit at forty feet." The mere utterance of the phrase has driven some of the best fishermen I know to tears.

Meanwhile, I am doing my best to catch a pass crab in the livewell. The fisherman on the bow typically has two, maybe three, casts to hook up before the fisherman in the back of the boat casts a live crab to the permit. Sometimes, you can miss the permit by ten or fifteen feet, and the fish will turn on a dime, chase the crab down, and crush it. It's been my experience that die-hard fly fishermen cringe at the thought that a live crab is more effective than a fly. Unfortunately, that's the norm, not the exception. But there are the times when the moon and the sun align in cosmic bliss, and a permit will go tail up and suck the fly down. When this happens, we call it karma. The guides call it luck. Personally, I don't care what they call it as long as I can land the damn fish. But, of course, hooking and landing a permit are two different ends of a fly rod.

Depending on the location, and the type of flats you are fishing, hooking a permit is just the first hurdle. Typically, when a big permit is finally hooked, it unapologetically beats feet across the flat at incredible speeds. The guide needs to pole his ass off or drop the engine quickly so the fisherman doesn't get spooled. The trick is to stay relatively close to the permit to put maximum pressure on the fish. If not, it's almost impossible to stop a big permit from going over the edge of the flat.

When you stop dribbling down your leg, the permit can be as deep as a hundred, sometimes two hundred, yards into the backing. The flat is littered with an array of obstacles that can and often do cause a tremendous amount of heartache. Corals, sea fans, crab traps, lobster traps, and other debris are just waiting to ruin your day. It's ninety-plus degrees, the humidity is thick enough to choke on, the sweat is running down your face, your shirt is soaked, and at some point, you stop listening to the guide and start mumbling the Lord's Prayer. You do your best to concentrate; you have long passed the point of any civil discourse with the guide, so why try. You attempt to convince yourself that the permit is bound to tire if you hang on long enough.

On the other hand, you concede that you will probably lose to the fish and have no one to blame but yourself. Then, out of nowhere, a 150-pound lemon shark comes screaming across the flat, closing in on your permit. Seconds later, the water turns red, and your fly line goes slack. The guide says something in Spanglish and turns away in disgust. Then you spend the remainder of the day trying to figure out if he's disgusted with you or the shark. At that point, all you can do is suck it up and move on. It's just another day in paradise. Next up!

So goes the day in a life of a die-hard permit fisherman.

Up the road, in the shack, the old man was sleeping again. He was sleeping on his face and the boy was sitting by him watching him. The old man was dreaming about the lions.

—ERNEST HEMINGWAY